Be an Inclusion Ally:

ABCs of LGBTQ+

Lisa Koenecke, M.S.
(she/her/hers)

Printed in the United States of America

ISBN: 979-8-6491-1449-3

Dedication

This book is dedicated to all of the LGBTQ+ trail blazers past, present and future who risked so much to be happy. I also honor the capital "A" Allies showing your rainbows, sharing your stories, and shifting mindsets to save lives. Thank you for being kind and generous (my favorite song by Natalie Merchant).

And most importantly, I dedicate this book to my wonderfully supportive wife, Angela! She is THE reason this book ever got published. Thanks for putting up with my 10 PM brainstorms and for thinking I'm funny, cuz I am. How did you find your way to me? Thank you for saying yes. I love you and Madi, too!

I also dedicate this book to TC, SV and to Jacob Thomas Koenecke. I wish I could have done more for you all!

For permission requests or for information about special discounts available for bulk purchases, sales promotions, fund-raising and educational needs contact:

Lisa Koenecke, LLC

Website and blog: www.LisaKoenecke.com
Email: Lisa@LisaKoenecke.com
LinkedIn: linkedin.com/in/lisakoenecke

Table of Contents

Preface   7

What People are Saying   9

A is for Ally   13

B is for Bisexual & Bystander & Binary   16

C is for Cisgender   18

D is for Diversity, Equity and Inclusion   20

E is for Equality vs. Equity   23

F is for Fun with Flags   25

G is for Geez, that's a lot of "G"s   30

H is for the Human Rights Campaign   32

I is for Intersectionality & Intersex   34

J is for Just Being Jazz   36

K is for Koenecke & Kevin Jennings   38

L is for Legislation & LGBTQ+   40

M is for Microagressions   43

N is for Non-Binary, Non-Conforming & Gender Neutral   45
Bathrooms

O is for Out   48

P is for Pride and PFLAG   51

Q is for Queer   53

R is for Riddle Scale (No Joke!)   55

S is for Show, Shift, Shape   58

T is for Transgender & The Trevor Project   60

U is for UUC and UCC   63

V is for Volunteering   66

W is for Welcoming Schools   69

X is for our XXIVth Letter!   71

Y is for You   73

Z is for Safe Zone Project Training   75

Calendar for LGBTQ+ Allies   77

Acknowledgements   83

About the Author   85

Preface

Why did I write this book? Thanks for asking. I wanted a quick and easy reference for anyone wanting to Be an Inclusion Ally, kinda like the title of the book. This book started with a weekly blog where I offered resources under each letter of the alphabet. A to Z resources for LGBTQ+ has been one of my favorite presentations to give to school counselors, so I wanted to capture all of those resources and put them into a book. This is where the ABCs come into the title. It's a primer, a quick and easy read, and it's funny, too!

According to my friend, Kimberly Neumaier, "Lisa does an amazing job of using each letter to provide readers with a step-by-step guide to a better understanding of the LGBTQ+ community. It is very inclusive and informative, plus it's an easy read. Highly recommended for adolescents & parents." THAT's why I wrote this book!

Please understand, I do not speak for all of the LGBTQ+ people in the world—or even for all of us in Wisconsin (I'm a born and bred cheesehead). I also realized that it is impossible to put every resource under every letter. I wanted to highlight the resources I thought would be most helpful for those entering the world of becoming an Inclusion Ally. For those of you wanting more resources or more content, let's connect. Perhaps we can rock and roll with Volume 2, or a podcast, or the next latest and greatest source of communication to come our way in the future.

Also, please note that this content is a snapshot in time, written to educate anyone not familiar with the ins and especially the outs of the LGBTQ+ community, as well as to help parents of young people who are finding their voice. It's also for anyone who wants to show more kindness and support in a world that really could use a big hug (I'm a hugger). This resource is a great starting point to educate yourself and others about how to be the best Ally you can be. There is so much more to say and so much more to learn from each other. I did my best to capture the framework for you, dear reader, to feel more confident in your support of our community. I hope you enjoy the quotes from famous LGBTQ+ people at the end of each chapter, they span the globe.

As you will read, I didn't know being gay was an option growing up in rural Wisconsin. My sister told me I was gay when I was 27. There were no gay role models for me. I had no resources and certainly no Internet growing up in the 1970s. Research says that some people know by age 3 who they truly are. I knew I liked toys made for boys. I hated dresses and I always liked being around girls. Did you know that I was forbidden to date a Catholic boy because we were Lutheran? Yep, true story. But they never said anything about a Catholic girl (Insert laugh track and rimshot here)!

All throughout high school and college I dated boys. When I moved to northern Virginia, I dated boys. In fact, one of them proposed to me on the Shenandoah River. Can you believe it? In college, I hung out with the female athletes. I was a summer camp director for 20 years. Hello girl power! Once my sister told me I was gay, I realized I could be my true self. Of course, that was after I cried for 24 hours continuously (never straight).

I wrote this book so individuals can celebrate who they truly are, and don't have to have a sibling tell you you're gay. This book is also a resource for people who are afraid to ask questions, or who don't want to offend anyone in the world of LGBTQ+. I use my true stories and LOTS of humor to ease you, dear reader, into the world of Inclusion.

My hope is that this book will be a support to whoever needs it and that it will, indeed, save lives!

Love and hugs, Lisa Koenecke (she/her/hers)

P.S. Did you know you can't lick your elbow?

P.P.S. If you just tried to lick your elbow, you are my people!

◆◆◆

"My silences had not protected me. Your silence will not protect you." ~ Audre Lorde, poet and so much more

Audre Lorde described herself as a "black, lesbian, mother, warrior, poet." In her writing, she frequently expressed her anger at the treatment of people of color, women, and LGBTQ folk. In her quote, she calls for others to express their anger. To many in the queer community, staying silent and in the closet felt like a safety blanket. Lorde encouraged them to step out into the light, telling them that the only true safety is in making yourself known and demanding the acceptance and respect that is your right.

What people are saying

◆◆◆

Lisa Koenecke is a powerhouse of information on issues around diversity, inclusion, and support of the LGBTQIA Community. She writes with wit and wisdom in a way that explains the concepts in an easy to understand format. Lisa approaches the teaching of vocabulary around LGBTQIA issues in a humorous, yet thoughtful way. Her book includes invaluable information and resources for anyone looking to learn more about these topics. I absolutely recommend this book to anyone who wants to understand LGBTQIA issues in greater depth. I give it 5 out of 5 hugs! ~ Sharon Hansen, MSE, LPC-IT (Doctoral Candidate)

◆◆◆

Be an Inclusion Ally: ABCs of LGBTQ is a practical guide to understanding and supporting family, friends, colleagues, anyone in the LBGTQ+ community. Written in an easy to follow, friendly style, this guide will provide concrete steps to those seeking to become an ally or an Ally. Ideal for personal learning, shared exploration, and instruction this is an invaluable resource. Not to be missed! Highly recommended. YA MC A ~ Val Edwards, Cornell University and lives in Oxford

◆◆◆

Lisa's book is an entertaining and engaging look at a wide variety of topics related to LGBTQ+. Lisa uses a lighthearted, story-oriented approach while sharing serious information. Her enthusiasm for the topic, combined with her experience in counseling are interwoven into each part of the book, making it more personal and inviting for readers. I invite others to enjoy and learn! ~ Shelley Joan Weiss USAF Retired Commander

◆◆◆

Fast paced, easy read, chock full of information, fun and funny. ~Gale F. Stone, Latin Goddess

◆◆◆

As a long-time middle-school educator, I've always strived to be an ally. It's never been more important. While I thought I had a pretty good handle on terminology and ways to support all students, Lisa's book added invaluable information and resources to my toolkit, and to be honest, clarified things that I hadn't realized needed clarification. Her style is conversational, funny and friendly, but what is persistently obvious is her passion for the importance of her message: all human beings deserve understanding, appreciation, respect, and support. There are many ways to provide this, big and small. I highly recommend this book; it is a relatively quick and easy read loaded with great useful information not just for educators, but, well…. for anyone, really. You'll find it to be worth your time. ~ Colleen Reilly, Retired teacher and super creative

◆◆◆

Lisa has an amazing way of taking the world, shaking it up, and tossing it on the table in such a way that anyone feels at ease. Whether it's having that ah-ha moment or reading the answer to a question you simply didn't know to ask, this book has it all FOR all. ~ Nanci Wilson, CUDE

◆◆◆

Lisa brings factual evidence to us to help us understand today's societal openness of expression towards identity and sexual preference. This is a must read for any age and any human interacting with other humans. The need for inclusion is a human right, not a "nice to have." We all must learn to be kind and accepting. This book is our first step. ~ Cindy Tschosik, NSA-Illinois

◆◆◆

I love the way you expressed your knowledge. I learned a lot through the pages; not only about the topic but about you as a person. Way to go! ~ Kimberly Neumaier

◆◆◆

W is for WOW, wonderful, wise, witty, warm hearted, well written!!! This is an invaluable resource for anyone who wants to learn, be inspired to be an Ally, teach others, and support others. Definitely written in Lisa's voice, with her insight, experience, knowledge and humor in full force!! ~ Lori Gibson

◆◆◆

As someone who has probably been more of a bystander than an Ally, this book has given me the knowledge, tools and ideas to step up and become an Ally. Lisa writes in such a fun and engaging manner that it was a joy to read. There are so many great links, quotes, definitions and anecdotes that I will use this as a primary resource in my future as an Ally! ~ Nicole Weisenberger

◆◆◆

Enlightened! Engaging! Energized! And now educated on all the nuances of being an ALLY! Thank you for putting this on paper in a form that resonates and can be referenced often! It's not a "read once and done" book! ~ Lisa Kazee, CUDE

◆◆◆

Absolutely fabulous. Quick, easy read, yet incredibly informative and educational. A great reference guide when you need to look something up! Great for adults and students! I will certainly use this book with my students, staff and families! Love it! ~ Bonnie Robbins, MS, NCC

◆◆◆

Learning to navigate the new ways of being is more than a letter and, as a human race, we need to start somewhere. In this book, you will find new words and concepts to help you learn about new ways of living in an approachable way. Read it cover to cover or one letter each week or day and you will expand your awareness, empathy, and compassion for people who are LGBTQ+ and their friends and families. It's not if, but when you will be touched by the LGBTQ+ community. This book will educate, connect and inspire you to see the facts of this emerging lifestyle. ~Holly Duckworth, CAE, CMP, LSP

LISA KOENECKE

A is for ally or is it for Ally?

Welcome to the first of 26 chapters on becoming a more inclusive LGBTQ+ Ally. This chapter will give you a very brief glimpse into the difference between a small "a" ally and a capital "A" Ally. Much more of this difference is included in the "S" chapter where I show you how to shift from ally to Ally. If you're reading this, you are already an Ally in my world. Awesome! You'll also find out I LOVE alliteration, and that I think I'm funny. Allow us, amigos, to advance. Ha, ha!

Have you ever had a girl say to you, "It's easier pretending to be a boy, than it is to be gay?" Well, I did, and that student changed my life. Throughout this book, you'll see real life examples of how you can be a capital "A" Ally to anyone who is marginalized.

I was a middle school counselor for many years and taught classroom lessons (LOVED it!). One lesson that made me stop in my tracks had to do with introducing the term ally to a group of 7th graders.

As I was getting my groove on to engage these adolescents, a small hand shot up to ask a question.

As I called on the student and loved her comment as I wrote the term ally on the board (yep, old school).

Student named Ally: *"Ms. Koenecke, that's my name."*

Me: *"Why, yes, it is."*

Student named Ally: *"So does that make me an automatic ally?"*

Me: *"What do you think?"*

Student named Ally: *"Absolutely! And now wherever I go, people will know that I'm an ally just by looking at my name, "Ally."*

Me: *"Ally, thanks for being an excellent ally, and students, that is also called a homonym."*

After this lesson, I reflected upon this homonym and how in later lessons we would discuss that homo means the same in Greek. So, if we are all the same in theory, why is there so much hate in the world? Answers? I wish I knew how to change hate to love.

What is an ally? Thanks for asking! If you are reading this, YOU are an Ally! Congrats and THANK YOU! An ally is a friend, a pal. In any marginalized community, an ally is a supporter that will stand up to discriminatory practices, using their position of strength as a member of the community not being marginalized. An ally acts when they hear or see anything offensive against a marginalized community. When they hear a homophobic, transphobic, or any slanderous joke, an ally stops the joke and stands up for any inequities. These are LGBTQ+ examples but can be used for other populations as well.

In the "S" chapter, I walk you through 3 ways, with examples, of how to become a capital "A" Ally. Feel free to skip ahead or allow the suspense to mount...your alternative. Aye?

There actually is a national Ally Week. Yep! It's in September and the Gay Lesbian Straight Education Network (GLSEN) offers free resources and ideas on how to boost your allyship. Here are some more resources for you about Ally Week.

- Note: Ally Week is in September. Check out my blog post about Ally Week.

In my very first podcast interview by Holly Duckworth of *Everyday Mindfulness*, Holly asked my advice on being an ally. My advice to her—and to you, dear reader—is to display a rainbow in your space. This could be a rainbow ribbon, a rainbow sticker, or even a rainbow flag to denote you are an ally. The rainbow is a symbol of unity for our LGBTQ+ community. Simply displaying this outward symbol of support and allyship will be a signal to anyone identifying in our marginalized community that you are a safe person and an ally. Depending on the culture and climate of your organization, you may be a beacon of hope to someone struggling with their identity. The simple act of solidarity can provide strength.

Thank you for saving a life!

Capital "A" Allies, at the end of the book you'll find a list of LGBTQs+ celebrations for you to mark on your calendars and to show you are an LGBTQ+ Ally! Thank you, again!

◆◆◆

"*Somebody*, your father or mine, should have told us that not many people have ever died of love. But multitudes have perished and are perishing every hour—and in the oddest places! —for the lack of it." ~ James Baldwin, author

◆◆◆

"Love him and let him love you. Do you think anything else under heaven really matters?" ~ James Baldwin

In his iconic, 1956 novel, Giovanni's Room, gay author James Baldwin makes a powerful statement about love. He proclaims that sex and gender don't matter; all that matters is that two people love each other. Nothing should stand in their way if they have love in their hearts. These words resonated with millions of people who felt like their emotions were invalid because of the gender of the object of their love. With this quote, Baldwin assured them that it didn't matter because love is love.

B is for Bisexual & Bystander & Binary

Bisexual

During my presentations on LGBTQ+ resources, I'm often asked "Why can't 'they' choose a side?" I typically answer their question with another question: "Why are you attracted to whomever you're attracted to?" It's not a choice. Let them Be!

As a middle school counselor, Bisexual was the number one term used (usually by females) to describe their identity if they had a very close female friend but didn't want to be called a lesbian. Perhaps in a young adolescent mind it left the door open to other opportunities. No matter what, I supported the student throughout their journey and felt honored to be a safe person they trusted.

What is the definition of Bisexual? Thanks for asking. According to Dictionary.com, Bisexual refers to *a person who is sexually attracted not exclusively to people of one particular gender.*

For more information, please check out the Bisexual Resource Center. Here you will find resources for youth and adults, a history of the organization and contact information. You'll find great information that will help you become an even better Ally.

Bystander

Bystander is the level before becoming an ally, or a small "a" ally. A bystander watches someone being bullied, attacked, or hurt and yet does nothing.

A bystander is the one who might not laugh at anti-LGBT+ jokes, but who remains silent. By not stopping the joke or remark, you are not an ally; you are merely a bystander standing on the sidelines. Saying something is the first step in becoming brave enough to fight against bullying; however, it is just a single step. In some spaces, it may feel like you would be the next in line for being attacked for standing up for someone else. And yet, without your voice, the unintended consequence is that those who are doing the bullying feel like they have carte blanche to continue their attacks. Because, after all, everyone thinks this is funny! By merely saying, "That's not funny," you shift the conversation and put others on alert that it's not o.k. to attack another person. Eleanor Roosevelt is quoted as saying, *"Do one thing every day that scares you."* I challenge you to make your one thing speaking up, even if it scares you! Be an Inclusion Ally!

One phrase that has benefited from bystanders becoming allies is the phrase, "That's So Gay." It wasn't long ago that you'd hear "That's So Gay" tossed around constantly. Thanks to a ton of hard work led by the Human Rights Campaign (HRC) & the National Education Association (NEA) teaching allies what to say when they hear "That's So Gay", coupled with the even harder work done by schools across the country, it's rare to hear that particular phrase these days. It's a true testament to the power of shifting from bystander to ally. We will explore more of the HRC's Welcoming Schools Campaign when we reach the letter "W" Until then, I encourage you to be brave! Be an Ally rather than just a bystander, please and thank you! Bravo!

Binary

If you are a mathematical kind of person (you know who you are!), then you know that Binary means of *two parts*. For the rest of us, not everyone identifies as male or female. Why does society continue to classify toys, clothing, etc. this way? Did you know you can even buy tools designated for females? They're the same as men's tools, but they have pink handles and are more expensive. (It's called **Non-binary**, or genderqueer, is a spectrum of gender identities that are not exclusively masculine or feminine— identities that are outside the gender binary. A non-binary gender is not associated with a specific gender expression, such as androgyny. Confused? Sorry.

The term gender binary describes the system in which a society allocates its members into one of two sets of gender roles, gender identities, and attributes based on the type of genitalia. Intersex people often identify anatomically as male or female; however, their innate sexual identity may be different. More on Intersex in chapter "I." Brilliant!

◆◆◆

"The next time someone asks you why LGBT Pride marches exist or why Gay Pride Month is June tell them 'A bisexual woman named Brenda Howard thought it should be.'" ~ Brenda Howard, activist

Brenda Howard is known as the "Mother of Pride." She was instrumental in organizing the first ever Pride marches: events that have become a vital part of the fight for acceptance. Howard was also one of the few activists to focus on rights for those who identified as bisexual or polyamorous: two groups that are often underrepresented in LGBTQ activism.

C is for Cisgender

The word Cisgender was a new term to me. Maybe it is a new term for you as well. Let's check it out collaboratively! Check! Cool!

Cis(gender): *Adjective that means "identifies as their sex assigned at birth" derived from the Latin word meaning "on the same side."* A cisgender/cis person is not transgender. *Cisgender* does not indicate biology, gender expression, or sexuality/sexual orientation. In discussions regarding trans issues, one would differentiate between women who are trans and women who aren't by saying *trans women* and *cis women*. Cis is not a "fake" word and is not a slur. Note that *cisgender* does not have an "ed" at the end.

As the term *transgender* has become increasingly prominent in our world, a contrasting term has also settled into the language. *Cisgender* (often shortened to cis) describes someone whose internal sense of gender corresponds with the sex the person had or was identified as having at birth. According to a 2016 *New York Times* article, it's estimated that approximately .6 % of people are transgender, so it follows that most people can be described as cisgender. If the pronouncement your mom heard at your birth—*It's a girl!* Or *It's a boy!* —still feels accurate, then you're cisgender.

I, Lisa Koenecke identify as cisgender. That is my gender identity. I also identify as a lesbian. That is my sexual orientation because I am attracted to women. Confused? It's o.k. if you are. I appreciate your willingness to learn with me. The use of the term cisgender took off around 2010. You haven't missed a lot!

In fact, according to the *Merriam Webster Dictionary* this word, *cisgender* was added in April 2017. See? You're right on track!

Cisgender/Cis is the opposite of *transgender*. Dang, look at your brain growing! Impressive!

Your call to action: When you are invited to a baby shower, or you have a baby present to give, please think about using neutral colors like green and yellow (Go Packers) rather than pink and blue. Gender reveal parties are all the rage; however, they might box the new human into a binary box. (You'll learn more about "binary" when we get to the letter G. Stay tuned!) I have pictures of me in dresses and wearing pink...back in the early 1970s, that's what was done. So, why did I like playing with my G.I. Joe and my Allis Chalmers tractor? Curious, isn't it? Apologies to my friend, Gale Stone for not having accuracy with Cis.

◆◆◆

From my Latin Scholar friend: *"Cis actually means on this side of, not on the same side. The Romans used cis and trans to refer to territory on either side of the Alps. Cisalpine Gaul and Transalpine Gaul are their specific words found in the writings of Julius Caesar."* ~ Gale Stone (GFS)

◆◆◆

"It is absolutely imperative that every human being's freedom and human rights are respected, all over the world." ~ Jóhanna Sigurðardóttir, Prime Minister

Jóhanna Sigurðardóttir, a former Icelandic Prime Minister and the first openly gay head of state, uttered these words during a speech at a 2014 Pride festival. In this speech, she was thankful that her native country was making strides towards acceptance and equal rights for LGBTQ people. However, she emphasized that until these rights are status quo all over the world, we cannot consider ourselves truly free. This marked one of the first calls from a head of state to make LGBTQ rights the standard worldwide.

◆◆◆

"When you are doing something that is right, you just do it and take care...Someone has to do this." ~ Alice Nkom, activist

Alice Nkom made history when she became the first female Cameroonian lawyer. In her time practicing law, she has dedicated her career to helping those who have been the victims of her country's harsh laws against homosexuality. The fight has been an uphill battle, as these types of laws are not uncommon in African countries. However, Nkom continues to fight, as she knows that her fight is just and right. With her work, she hopes to usher in a new era for the rights of the LGBTQ population in Cameroon.

D is for Diversity, Equity & Inclusion

How interesting! When I typed "DEI" into a search engine, what do you think was the first thing that popped up? If you said, DEI, a Greek national electric company, I would say, "OPA!" to you. Next, I found Dale Earnhardt, Inc. Go cars! Finally, I found what I was hoping for: Diversity, Equity & Inclusion. This term is being used in workplaces to raise awareness of our individual needs as well as to highlight the benefits of greater diversity in our workplaces. It's common for organizations to hire people who look and think like people already working for them—people who live, look, and work like they do. That has certainly been my truth. As a lesbian, I often feel like I am THE diversity in the room, so I have used that as an opportunity to educate those around me with lots & LOTS of rainbows! Delightful!

What is the meaning of diversity and inclusion in the workplace? Thanks to our friends at SHRM (Society for Human Resource Management) for their definition. **Inclusion**, while closely related, is a separate concept from **diversity**. SHRM defines **inclusion** as *"the achievement of a work environment in which all individuals are treated fairly and respectfully, have equal access to opportunities and resources, and can contribute fully to the organization's success"* (Mar 6, 2014). If you want to learn more about building a business case for diversity and inclusion, please go to SHRM's website for a great resource. www.shrm.com and search for Diversity. Or, again, you can hire me, I have a Diversity and Inclusion certification from Cornell University.

As a school counselor, diversity training was always a part of back-to-school pre-service work. We might have used the terms "Celebrate Diversity" or made bulletin boards to reflect our student body. I bring up the school examples because my work at a university involves training the next generation of school counselors. In addition, I bring this message to the business world through my speaking and consulting business, Lisa Koenecke, LLC. Learn more at www.lisakoenecke.com.

One of the first steps in raising Diversity, Equity & Inclusion in your organization is to raise awareness through a company- or school-wide definition of what DEI means to you. A great example to get you started on this path comes from the University of Michigan and their website:

Defining Diversity, Equity, and Inclusion "At the University of Michigan, our dedication to academic excellence for the public good is inseparable from our commitment to diversity, equity, and inclusion. It is central to our mission as an educational institution to ensure that each member of our community has full opportunity to thrive in our environment, for we believe that diversity is key to individual flourishing, educational excellence and the advancement of knowledge. **Diversity**: We commit to increasing diversity, which is expressed in a myriad of forms, including race and ethnicity, gender and gender identity, sexual orientation, socioeconomic status, language, culture, national origin, religious commitments, age, (dis)ability status and political perspective.

Equity: We commit to working actively to challenge and respond to bias, harassment, and discrimination. We are committed to a policy of equal opportunity for all persons and do not discriminate on the basis of race, color, national origin, age, marital status, sex, sexual orientation, gender identity, gender expression, disability, religion, height, weight, or veteran status.

Inclusion: We commit to pursuing deliberate efforts to ensure that our campus is a place where differences are welcomed, different perspectives are respectfully heard and where every individual feels a sense of belonging and inclusion. We know that by building a critical mass of diverse groups on campus and creating a vibrant climate of inclusiveness, we can more effectively leverage the resources of diversity to advance our collective capabilities."

Robert Sellers, University of Michigan's Chief Diversity Officer, often has emphasized the importance of considering all three topics – diversity, equity, and inclusion – which he likened to various aspects of attending a dance:

"Diversity is where everyone is invited to the party."

"Equity means that everyone gets to contribute to the playlist."

"And inclusion means that everyone has the opportunity to dance."

Your call to action on Diversity, Equity & Inclusion (DEI) is to make sure your registration forms, artwork on the walls, and actions are in alignment with an Inclusive environment for all. Ask your human resources person/people if they have the DEI certification. And while it would be amazing for you all to adopt a DEI definition and policy, you know you can always start with a rainbow on your lanyard or a rainbow sticker on your desk.

Let's all dance together!

Done and Done!

◆◆◆

"Every LGBTQ+ refugee has a unique situation—but the fear and pain they endured before coming to Canada is universal." ~ Arsham Parsi, activist

Arsham Parsi, an Iranian refugee living in Canada in exile, has made it his mission to help LGBTQ people living in Iran: a nation where acts of homosexuality are punishable by flogging or even death. In the above quotation, Parsi seeks the assistance of LGBTQ people living in Western nations, providing a powerful reminder that while things are slowly improving in the west, there are still queer people all over the world who live every day afraid for their very lives.

E is for Equality vs. Equity

Let's look at the difference between the terms *equality* and *equity*. By the Dictionary.com definition, **equality** *is ensuring individuals or groups of individuals are not treated differently or less favorably, on the basis of their specific protected characteristic, including areas of race, gender, disability, religion or belief, sexual orientation and age* (check out that *Enumeration!*). While **equity** means *the quality of being fair or impartial* (dictionary.com). These terms can be confusing, so you'll often see different analogies to help make the difference a bit easier to understand. Which analogy is your favorite?

My favorite is the shoe analogy from Naheed Dosani: "Equality is giving everyone a shoe. Equity is giving everyone a shoe that fits."

I would even go a bit further to add *inclusion* to the shoe analogy, meaning that everyone has a shoe that fits, the shoe is comfortable and matches their sense of style. Who wants a rainbow pair of shoes? The first time I heard the shoe analogy to represent Equality vs. Equity was at a training called "Courageous Conversations." This training was early in my school counseling career and reminded me of growing up with an uncle who had polio. His physical limitations were perhaps equal to those needing the specified parking space, but his brilliant mind gave him equity in his place of work among the other able-bodied engineers. In fact, he was a very successful manager and he taught me how to play chess. Thanks, Uncle Norbie!

Perhaps you have seen the analogy of the people watching a ball game and there are three boxes. Everyone is standing (or in a wheelchair) on a different box trying to see over the fence. Equality is that each person has a box upon which to stand/sit. Equity is that the tallest person can see over the fence without a box, the middle person has one box and can now see over the fence and the third person is standing on two boxes in order to see over the fence. Have you included a ramp for wheelchairs? Another way to approach this scenario is to consider removing the fence all together. Let's consider taking away barriers in order to promote equity. Eh?

Personally, I don't like using the word *versus* in between *Equality* and *Equity*. These two goals shouldn't be seen as a competition. Depending upon where you are in your cultural awareness journey, or how your life experiences have shaped the lens through which you view the world, I might suggest that we all strive for success for ALL! When you're just starting your journey, equality is a good place to start. A rising tide lifts all boats.

Equity is good for ALL. Think about those registration forms we all complete. In schools, by asking for <u>adult 1</u> or <u>caregiver 1</u> rather than "<u>mom</u>" and "<u>dad</u>," you are now including grandparents, foster parents, or another relative caring for that student. Oh, and not everyone is a husband or a wife or a mom or a dad! That plays out in the business world when you make the switch to ask for <u>applicant 1</u> and <u>applicant 2</u> rather than <u>husband</u> and <u>wife</u> or <u>male</u> and <u>female</u>. Cheryl Wheeler is a folk singer and songwriter who just happens to sing one of my favorite songs called, "Gandhi & Buddha." In her live version, she introduces the song sharing how she was happy to finally be able to marry her wife. Then she apologizes—tongue in cheek—for how our gay marriages have ruined all the heterosexual marriages. In other words, by giving everyone the right to marry, whose marriage has that hurt? AND now my wife and I have access to the 1,100 protections and laws that heterosexual couples have enjoyed throughout time, while not taking a single protection away from hetero couple's marriages. Win-win when love wins! Excellent!

So, in terms of equality, the Lesbian and Gay world can equally get married as a man and a woman can. On the other hand, equity is felt in some areas more than others. My wife and I chose to live in Madison, Wisconsin, which for the most part is a very welcoming city. It's nice when I call to make an appointment for my wife that I only get asked a couple of questions. I'm not sure that if we were a male and a female couple I would be asked the same questions, however I don't get push-back or a negative reaction that might occur in some less-equitable areas. That said, the majority of the time when we go out to dinner as a couple, we still get asked if we want separate checks, even if we've been holding hands across the table throughout our meal. I don't get it. Your call to action is to do something EXTRA to make things more equitable in your workspace! Stand up for those without a voice. Take the time to educate someone needing that lesson on how to treat people! Think about this...intelligence is distributed equally, but opportunity is not!

◆ ◆ ◆

"Equality means more than passing laws. The struggle is really won in the hearts and minds of the community, where it really counts." ~ Barbara Gittings, activist

Barbara Gittings is known for being an American activist fighting on behalf of the LGBTQ population. In her most well-known fight she took on a Goliath: the United States government. She picketed to stop them from barring LGBTQ applicants from employment. However, as she states in the above quote, her greatest wish was not for laws to pass, but for true acceptance and equality.

F is for Fun with Flags

Fantastic! Finally, Fun with Flags! For you "Big Bang Theory" Fans, Forgive me. Fabulous! Ok, enough of the alliteration. Let's get to the facts. With our journey into LGBTQ+ frequently asked questions, today we will discover the plus (+) that often gets put at the end of LGBTQ+. The + includes many identities, and I am focusing on their flags for you to fathom.

I dedicate this Fun with Flags chapter to:

- Gilbert Baker: Designer and creator of the original 8-stripe Pride flag in 1978;
- Harvey Milk: After his assassination, demand for the Baker Pride flag soared;
- Monica Helms: Designer of the Transgender Pride flag in 1999;
- The city of Philadelphia: For adding Queer People of Color (QPOC) to the ROY G BIV flag in June 2017; and,
- Daniel Quasar: Designer of the 2018 Progress Pride flag.

A shout out to Target for their celebration of PRIDE month every June. Last year, I was able to pick up a variety of small LGBT flags that I posted in my office. I love the dollar section at Target during PRIDE month, which often includes items featuring the Rainbow (Gay), pink/blue/white (Transgender), and a pink/blue/purple (Bisexual) flags during Pride month. Go there in June! More about PRIDE in the "P" chapter.

This is a nice summary of Gilbert Baker's original flag from 1978. Thank you, Gilbert Baker Foundation! I did reach out to them and thanked them personally. Fun!

The 8 color flag

Hot pink	Sex
Red	Life
Orange	Healing
Yellow	Sunlight
Green	Nature
Turquoise	Magic/Art
Indigo	Serenity
Violet	Spirit

Today, the hot pink and the turquoise stripes have been dropped because it was difficult to find pink and turquoise material in the late 1970s, so here is what we see most often today:

Now, let's jump into the plus (+) of LGBTQ+ along with the other flags and who they represent. Thank you, Live Loud Graphics!

This graphic from Live Loud Graphics (used with permission) gives more insight into the different terminology of the LGBTQ+ community and the different flags that help give a voice to our individual identities. There may be groups you've never heard of—that's fantastic! There may be groups that give voice to an identity you've experienced and didn't realize there were others like you—that's exciting! The purpose isn't to divide an already marginalized group; it really is to highlight all the different facets that make up our community and to celebrate each one. There may be intersectionality happening here as well. No labels, just education. You'll learn more about intersectionality in chapter "I."

LGBT Community Terminology and Flags

Sexual, romantic, and gender identities are very personal and often change from person to person. The information below is is simply a general guide to some popular LGBT community terms. When dealing with these terms it is important to remember that gender identity, romantic attraction, and sexuality are independent of each other. Some of these term can be used in a derogatory way and care should be used when speaking with someone about their gender identity, sexuality, or romantic attraction. It is always a best practice to ask the person which terms they prefer.

Sexual Orientation
The way a person defines their sexual preferences.

Gender Identity
The way a person expresses their personal feelings about where they fall on the spectrum of genders between male and female.

Romantic Attraction
the feeling that causes people to desire intimacy, monogamy, and/or sexual activities with another person.

Sexual Orientation	Gender Identity	Romantic Attraction
Gay	**Gender Fluid**	**Aromantic**
Gay Bear	**Androgynous**	**Greyromantic**
Androphilia	**Drag / Feather**	**Lithromantic**
Lesbian	**Genderqueer**	**Demiromantic**
Lipstick Lesbian	**Gender Binary**	**Relationship**
Gynephilia	**Gender Non-Binary**	**Polyamorous**
Asexual	**Hermaphrodite**	
Demisexual	**Intersexual**	
Autosexual	**Neutrois**	
Bisexual	**Transexual**	
Pansexual	**Transgender**	
Polysexual	**Two-Spirit**	
Skoliosexual	**Trigender**	
Straight Ally		

Live Loud Graphics -
Education is the cure for homophobia

27

This next flag might be known to some as the Philly Flag. In 2017, the city of Philadelphia adopted the Gilbert Baker flag and included a black and a brown stripe to include Queer People of Color. It was even highlighted in the Oprah Magazine. Thank you, Oprah, for helping us learn more about our flags. Fabulous! (Said in Oprah's voice, of course!)

Fast forward to 2018 and Daniel Quasar, the creator of the Progress Pride Flag. I LOVE this flag! After talking with Daniel on Facebook (Yep, totally cool!), I'm delighted to share the background on the Progress Flag in Daniel's own words. Check out his website at quasar.digital.com where you can buy more cool Progress Flag merchandise. A portion of the sales help another non-profit organization. Nicely done, Daniel! And thank you!

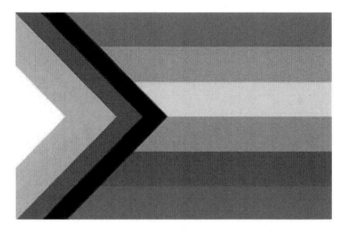

"When the Pride flag was recreated in 2017 and 2018 to include both black/brown stripes, as well as the trans stripes, I wanted to see if there could be more emphasis in the design of the flag to elevate its meaning. The 6 stripe LGBTQ flag should be separated from the newer stripes because of their difference in meaning, as well as to shift focus and emphasis to what is important in our current community climate. The main section of the flag (background) includes the traditional 6 stripe LGBTQ flag as seen in its most widely used form so as not to take away from its original meaning (seen above). The trans flag stripes and marginalized community stripes were shifted to the Hoist of the flag and given a new arrow shape. The arrow points to the right to show forward movement, while being along the left edge shows that progress still needs to be made. Background: LGBTQ 6 full sized color stripes representing life (red), healing (orange), sunlight (yellow), nature (green), harmony/peace (blue), and spirit (purple/violet) Hoist: 5 half sized stripes representing trans and non-binary individuals (light blue, light pink, white), marginalized POC communities (brown, black), as well as those living with AIDS and the stigma and prejudice surrounding them, and those who have been lost to the disease (black)." ~ Daniel Quasar

◆◆◆

"It takes no compromise to give people their rights ...it takes no money to respect the individual. It takes no political deal to give people freedom. It takes no survey to remove repression." ~ Harvey Milk, politician, and activist

◆◆◆

"If you help elect more gay people, that gives a green light to all who feel disenfranchised a green light to move forward." ~ Harvey Milk

When Harvey Milk became the first openly gay person elected to public office in California, he became the face of the push to put more LGBTQ people in positions of power. In this quotation, he stresses that doing so will not only monumental for those in the queer community who don't feel represented; it will also empower anyone who feels disenfranchised by those who are supposed to represent them.

G is for Geez, that's a lot of "G"s

You've most likely seen the acronym "LGBT" to refer to the rainbow of people in the Lesbian Gay Bisexual Transgender community. You might see other letters added like "Q" (Questioning/Queer), "I" (Intersex...wait until we get to the chapter on the letter "I"), "A" (Ally), and maybe a "+" sign to include many others. This chapter is brought to you today by the letter "G" (Cue the Sesame Street music)! Thank you, Grover!

"Gay" back in the day was a happy term. Gay old times. Remember that? Then the term morphed into a negative slur, like "That's so Gay!" One of my favorite teaching tools comes from a Public Service Announcement created by GLSEN (Gay Lesbian Straight Education Network). Wanda Sykes has an excellent 30 second YouTube clip that is great! Check out the Resources link on my website LisaKoenecke.com (under THE BOOK tab) for a link to the video.

I have used this Wanda Sykes YouTube clip to represent how we can all address hate speech. I am not advocating putting others down to make your point, but rather to remind people to Think B4 You Speak. GLSEN also has a FREE 55 page Think B4 You Speak guide you can download on your own to help address anti-LGBT language in grades 6-12 classrooms. GLSEN is my Go-To for Gay Goods/resources. Lots of "G"s.

Please check out GLSEN's website for free resources, to register your school for educational materials and to mark your calendars for LGBTQ+ awareness weeks. I have also included this calendar of the events for you at the end of the book.

Gender has been a term bubbling to the surface in the LGBTQ+ world for years. Gender reveal parties (I am not a fan), Gender Identity, Gender Queer, and Gender Expression are just a few examples. An excellent resource on all things Gender is Gender Spectrum which *"helps to create gender sensitive and inclusive environments for all children and teens."* Gobs of resources for your gender-related questions! Go there!

Geez, that is a lot of "G"s—and I'm not done yet! Research states that by having one safe adult in a school, teens identifying somewhere on the LGBTQ+ rainbow will believe in themselves and their attempts at suicide reduce by 40%. I use this statistic in my TEDx talk "Allies Save Lives." Check out GLSEN's Research! Another Great resource is starting a Gay Straight Alliance (GSA) or Gender Spectrum Alliance in your school. Check out the GSA Network. If you're in Wisconsin, my favorite is GSAFE (Gay Straight Alliance for Safe Schools) tell them Lisa (Lady Rainbow) sent you!

If you're not in a school and you're still reading this, you might offer to mentor at a school, or make sure your place of work is "G" friendly (Gay, Gender non-conforming, Gender neutral bathrooms, Gender Expression, etc.) Check out the Diversity, Equity, and Inclusion resources at your company. If you don't have any...Call me! I can be your Go-To consultant! I'm a genuine Diversity & Inclusion Certified professional speaker from Cornell University! Great!

Gender Identity books: There are lots out there! Two excellent examples are *I am Jazz* by Jessica Herthel & *Introducing Teddy* by Jessica Walter. Watch for my upcoming book about a beaver and a homecoming queen from this speaker in the rainbow sneakers!

Your goal after reading this is to investigate one or more of the resources mentioned or find your own. I'd love to hear what you find the most helpful!

- GLSEN for gobs of resources

- Gender Spectrum

- GSA Network

- GSAFE (Wisconsin)

I am grateful and filled with gratitude for your readership, and dare I say I would be giddy if you shared these resources? Gracias! How many "G" did you gather in this chapter?

◆◆◆

"I'm living by example by continuing on with my career and having a full, rich life, and I am incidentally gay." ~ Portia DeRossi, actor

H is for the Human Rights Campaign (HRC)

My first thought was to give you information on heterosexual vs. homosexual. Then I read an interesting article I had to share with you, along with giving a shout out to the Human Rights Campaign—one of my favorite organizations—and to my friend, Dr. Vinnie Pompei, who works tirelessly for our collective rights. Hooray!

HRC is a wonderful organization. Directly from their website (notice I didn't say straight from their website? Ha ha!): *"The Human Rights Campaign represents a force of more than 3 million members and supporters nationwide. As the largest national lesbian, gay, bisexual, transgender and queer civil rights organization, HRC envisions a world where LGBTQ people are ensured of their basic equal rights, and can be open, honest and safe at home, at work and in the community."*

October 10, 2019, marked HRC's exclusive broadcasting partnership with CNN. CNN and HRC hosted the first ever Equity Town Hall, inviting 9 of the top 2020 Democratic presidential candidates to discuss LGBT issues. Just the fact that we are seeing these discussions and advocacy in my lifetime gives me hope for the future. For more information, Google the "9 Takeaways from CNN's Equality Forum," or check out the Resources link on my website LisaKoenecke.com (under THE BOOK tab) for a link to the video. For those of you wanting a chuckle, watch Saturday Night Live's take on the CNN LGBTQ Forum. You'll need to watch some of the original footage to understand the SNL skits. Thank you, CNN & HRC & SNL!

More from HRC, *"This historic town hall event, entitled Power of Our Pride, is set to take place on the eve of the 31st annual National Coming Out Day, a celebration of coming out as lesbian, gay, bisexual, transgender, queer (LGBTQ) or as an ally. The first National Coming Out Day was held on October 11, 1988 on the first anniversary of the National March on Washington for Lesbian and Gay Rights as a way of celebrating the power of coming out and promoting a safe world for LGBTQ individuals to live truthfully and openly. (HRC.org)"*

Oh, and my friend, Dr. Vinnie Pompei? He is a rockstar working for HRC. He and I met in San Diego at The Center for Excellence in School Counseling and Leadership *Supporting Students—Saving Lives* conference. One of the best ways to grow your knowledge is to attend Vinnies' HRC's Time to Thrive Conference. I was fortunate to speak at the conference and hope to speak there again. This is where I met Jazz Jennings! Hold on for chapter "J."

One of my early LGBTQ consultations was with a private Catholic high school. I was asked to help their school counseling department create a safe and welcoming environment. We discussed using rainbows as a universal sign designating the school counseling office as a safe zone for those identifying as LGBTQ. After thinking about what the Catholic Diocese would think about rainbows, that idea was squashed. We had to go back to the drawing board. I mentioned the Human Rights Campaign equality sticker. Rather than the blue and yellow colors in the HRC equality sign sticker, this school decided to use their school colors with their school mascot behind the equal sign. Use your imagination, but please know you might be saving a life through your efforts!

Head on over to HRC's website for resources, information, and swag! Hooray!

◆◆◆

"I hate the word homophobia. It's not a phobia. You're not scared. You're an asshole."
~ Morgan Freeman, actor

I is for Intersectionality & Intersex

This chapter goes out to Dr. Erin Mason in Georgia. When I was seeking advice on what topic I should write about for the letter "I," Erin said, "Intersectionality" a fairly new term to me in 2017. So, what is intersectionality? Let's find out, and as always...thanks for asking! I love you, Dr. Erin Mason (not in a romantic way).

According to Merriam Webster: Intersectionality is: *"the complex, cumulative manner in which the effects of different forms of discrimination combine, overlap, or intersect."*

It's a lot to take in, so let's break it down. While the concept has been around since the late 1980s, intersectionality is a word that's new to many of us. In fact, *Intersectionality* was just added to the Merriam Webster dictionary in April 2017. It's used to refer to the way that the effects of different forms of discrimination (such as racism, sexism, and homophobia) can combine, overlap, and yes, intersect, especially in the experiences of marginalized people or groups.

The term was coined by legal scholar Kimberlé Crenshaw in a 1989 essay that asserts that "antidiscrimination law, feminist theory, and antiracist politics all fail to address the experiences of black women because of how they each focus on only a single factor." Crenshaw writes that "because the intersectional experience is greater than the sum of racism and sexism, any analysis that does not take intersectionality into account cannot sufficiently address the particular manner in which Black women are subordinated." I am super proud to say she has deep connections to my home state of Wisconsin. She spent time as a University of Wisconsin Law School Fellow and a law clerk to the Wisconsin Supreme Court! I sure hope to meet her one day and thank her in person!

Though originally applied only to the ways that sexism and racism combine and overlap, *intersectionality* has come to include other forms of discrimination as well, such as those based on class, sexuality, and ability. Considering complexities in the LGBTQ+ spectrum, it becomes more clear as to how difficult it is to separate or compartmentalize just one portion of our lives. We have to consider the entire individual to be able to truly help them.

So, there you have it from the technical side of things. As a white, cisgender, able-bodied, middle-class individual, I realize my privilege. Yet I am a *woman* who also identifies as *gay*, which is my intersectionality. I encourage you to continue to educate yourself on supporting all populations, considering each person's intersectionality so you don't inadvertently force someone to hide a piece of themselves. Our goal should always be to support the whole person. Indubitably.

Intersex (warning, this is rated PG for anatomical words)

Let's talk about another letter "I" word, *Intersex*. Have you heard of this term? From the Intersex Society of North America "Intersex" is a general term used for a variety of conditions in which a person is born with a reproductive or sexual anatomy that doesn't seem to fit the typical definitions of female or male. For example, a person might be born appearing to be female on the outside but having mostly male-typical anatomy on the inside. Or a person may be born with genitalia that seem to be in-between the usual male and female types—for example, a girl may be born with a noticeably large clitoris or lacking a vaginal opening, or a boy may be born with a notably small penis, or with a scrotum that is divided so that it has formed more like labia. Or a person may be born with mosaic genetics, meaning some of her cells have XX chromosomes and some of them have XY. You may think being born intersex is pretty uncommon, so why do we even need know about this? Thanks for asking!

At one point in my research, I read there were more people born intersex than people born with cleft palates. The Intersex Society of North America (ISNA) is devoted to systemic change to end shame, secrecy, and unwanted genital surgeries for people born with an anatomy that someone decided is not standard for male or female. When a baby is born Intersex, the parent may be making a decision regarding completing genital surgery that isn't in sync with that child's identity when they grow up. Wouldn't it be better to let the child develop into their own identity?

Now you can see why I am not a fan of gender reveal parties! Consider gifts of something other than pink or blue. You don't know what the details of a family might be, and the small act of using gender neutral colors like green, yellow, or purple might just help a new parent feel better about their new baby. Plus, green and yellow are the Green Bay Packers colors! Go Pack Go! When in doubt, give cash. It's green. See? It's easy to give gender-neutral gifts. You're welcome!

◆◆◆

"AIDS is a plague—numerically, statistically and by any definition known to modern public health—though no one in authority has the guts to call it one." ~ Larry Kramer, activist

The AIDS epidemic, which reached its peak in the 80s and 90s, was a vital moment for the queer community. Gay men were the group most ravaged by the disease, and the most feared and hated group because of it. Larry Kramer was a vocal advocate for those suffering from AIDS and continued to speak out until his death on May 28, 2020, about the failure of our society to help and protect those who are suffering.

J is for Just being Jazz

This chapter is dedicated to Jazz Jennings. *Jazz* introduces herself in her own words by sharing, "*My name is Jazz and I'm transgender which means that I was assigned male at birth but was a girl right from the start. I expressed myself as a girl to my family by gravitating towards dolls, dresses, sparkles, and everything feminine. I didn't just like girly objects, but I heavily insisted that I WAS a girl. All my family wanted was my happiness and they assured that by providing me unconditional love and support. As kindergarten approached, I would be heading to a new school and a fresh start was coming. We took this opportunity to begin my transition as a girl. I finally blossomed into my authentic self. Although this seems like it might've been the end of my story of me finally becoming a girl, it was only the beginning...*"

I was lucky enough to meet Jazz in Portland, Oregon, at the Human Rights Campaign's *Time to Thrive* conference. She was coming back from Voodoo Donuts with her mom as we were heading out to get our own donuts. She was poised and gracious when I told her how proud I was of her. And of course, I had to hug her! Why didn't I get a picture with her? Arrrggghhh! That was before selfies were popular. Jeepers!

Times are changing, but I still can't imagine the strength, courage, and adult support Jazz had and still has to this day. She knew she was born in the wrong body when she was 6 years old. When I was 6, I was playing with my tractors and my G.I. Joe. Read on to see how Jazz and Wisconsin crossed paths.

In 2015, the *Wisconsin State Journal* reported on the reading of the book *I Am Jazz* in the small Wisconsin town of Mount Horeb, population 7,421. The article encapsulates the issues so well that I decided to include it:

MOUNT HOREB — *In a turnout that stunned organizers, nearly 600 people filled the library here Wednesday night to hear a public reading of a children's book about a transgender girl, with many in the crowd expressing strong support for a local family with a transgender child. The library event — and another reading at the high school on Wednesday morning that drew about 200 — followed the cancellation last week of the reading of the book I Am Jazz at the Mount Horeb Primary Center, a public elementary school where a 6-year-old student had just transitioned from a boy to a girl. School staff said they sought to read the book to the girl's classmates to help them understand what was happening to a fellow student, and to help the girl feel safe and accepted. The school canceled the reading after a conservative Florida-based group threatened legal action.*

The centerpiece of the library program was the reading of I Am Jazz *by its co-author Jessica Herthel, who flew in from California to support the family. As a straight parent, Herthel said she wrote her book with Jazz Jennings, a transgender girl who stars in a TLC reality show, in part because she felt there were not enough resources for parents like her to teach their children about acceptance. She said she was overwhelmed by the community response in Mount Horeb. "I think it's a barometer of where we're at as a society," she said in an interview. "I think we're more ready to hear about this issue from a child's perspective, because we know a child isn't making a political statement or rebelling against society. Kids don't know not to tell the truth, and we're getting more comfortable with that idea." "When people take the time to read the book, they realize that* I Am Jazz *is about identity — who you are. Not sex — who you are attracted to. And the book's message of 'Be who you are, no matter what' applies to all children," Herthel said.*

Two Eleanor Roosevelt quotes come to mind when I think about Jazz's journey: *"Do one thing every day that scares you"* and *"People grow through experience if they meet life honestly and courageously. This is how character is built."* Jazz knew who she was at a young age. She is a courageous trailblazer.

Want to learn more about this amazing person? You can read her children's book *I Am Jazz*, you could watch her on YouTube, or check out *"I am Jazz"* on the TV channel TLC. In 2017, the Tonner Doll Company announced plans to produce the first transgender doll. Please notice we use the term transgender and not transgendered. More on that in the "T" chapter.

In our everyday lives, you will hear more people identify as transgender (or trans) and becoming their true selves—comfortable in their skin and their bodies perhaps for the first time in their lives. You'll have multiple opportunities to embrace and enhance your allyship, and I invite you to turn to me with any questions along the way. Ask questions and share resources like this book with others. Please check out the book *I Am Jazz*, or buy it and donate it to a school library. The kids will be Jubilant! Especially if your middle name is Jubilee!

◆◆◆

"Openness may not completely disarm prejudice, but it's a good place to start." ~ Jason Collins, professional athlete

In 2014, Jason Collins made history by becoming the first male professional athlete to publicly identify himself as gay. After his announcement, a flood of other queer athletes began declaring their sexuality, revealing to the world that some of our greatest sports figures are, in fact, LGBTQ. This was a milestone for the fight for equality because, as Collins says, being open about sexual orientation is an important step towards ending prejudice.

K is for Koenecke & Kevin Jennings

I, Lisa Koenecke, was in the closet for so long because I didn't know that being gay (and ultimately happy) was an option. Being raised Missouri Synod Lutheran didn't offer a great deal of hope for females, let alone, females loving other females. My mom and I used to volunteer to clean our church on Saturdays. I would always volunteer to go with my mom for the main reason of being able to stand in the pulpit and "preach" whatever was on my mind. You might want to sit down (if you aren't already) for this next part...I wanted to marry a pastor. Not a female pastor, but a male one. YIKES! What was I thinking? Oh right! That's what was modeled for me. As I grew older, I gained more confidence in myself as a strong, independent female. After all, my mother had named me Lisa after Eileen Fulton's character on the soap opera "*As the World Turns*," because she wanted me to be a strong female. Careful what you wish for, right?

When I realized that I could be the pastor and that I didn't have to rely on a man, I wanted to volunteer at church to be an usher. All my uncles were, so why not me? It was then that my relationship with the church changed my views. My aunt was the treasurer at our 100-member tiny church on the hill. I was related to half of the congregation. In fact, if our carload of cousins were late to Saturday/Sunday school, they would wait for us to start so they'd have enough kids to hold class. When I told my aunt that I wanted to be an usher, she told me that women weren't allowed to be ushers. WHAT?!?! I'm shaking my head as I write this. My church had let me down. Now what to do? I'll tell you in the next paragraph.

I went to college, hung out with all the female athletes, and worked at a summer camp! Too bad I didn't know what coming out meant my freshman year at UW-LaCrosse. October 11th thirty-one years ago would have been the first National Coming OUT Day. I wonder how my life would have turned out differently if I had been true to myself? Who would have thought thirty-one years ago that there would be a presidential debate focused solely on LGBTQ+ issues? We've come a long way in the past thirty-one years, and yet, we have so much further to go. Keep on reading!

K is also for Kevin Jennings

Now, we will pay homage to Kevin Jennings who founded the Gay, Lesbian, Straight Education Network (GLSEN). Oh, and he was a school counselor! Yep! That's right! A school counselor just like yours truly. He is just one of the famous LGBTQ+ activists we can learn about during October which is always National LGBTQ History Month. Kool!

Kevin, as I like to call him, went to Harvard—no big deal—and in 1988 he started America's first Gay-Straight Alliance (GSA) at the Concord Academy in Massachusetts.

Today, there are thousands of GSAs in our schools. There are other names for GSAs including Gender Sexuality Alliance and many others. Read on to learn more about Kevin Jennings in these excerpts from the National Education Association's Cindy Long in her article An Interview with *Kevin Jennings, Founder of GLSEN: Safe Schools for Everyone:*

"When Kevin Jennings taught history in Rhode Island, he saw students verbally bullied and harassed to the breaking point. It reminded him of the torment of the endless name-calling he suffered when he was in school. But when the bullying among his students began to turn physical, he decided he had to do something to make school a safer place for everyone. That's when he founded the Gay, Lesbian and Straight Education Network (GLSEN).

GLSEN is a national education organization focused on ensuring safe schools for all students. Established nationally in 1995, GLSEN works with educators, students, and the community to help children learn to respect and accept all people, regardless of sexual orientation or gender identity and expression."

I have used GLSEN for numerous resources and applaud the organization for celebrating our community, especially the youth. Here is my article on GLSEN, "Geez, That's a lot of "G's." The "S" in GLSEN stands for straight—without our straight allies, we would be facing an uphill battle every day! In 2015, I was a national semi-finalist for GLSEN's National Educator of the Year...how's that for a fun fact? I didn't win, but it was a huge honor to be nominated. Kool!

◆◆◆

"Never be bullied into silence. Never allow yourself to be made a victim. Accept no one's definition of your life; define yourself." ~ Harvey Fierstein, actor and activist

◆◆◆

"This world would be a whole lot better if we just made an effort to be less horrible to one another." ~ Ellen Page, actor and activist

L is for Legislation & LGBTQ+

Let's give it up for the letter "L!" What a Lovely Letter that has Literally Labelled Lisa (me) as a strong Lady! As I mentioned earlier, my mother named me after a soap opera star...true story. Eileen Fulton played the character Lisa Grimaldi on *As the World Turns*." Lisa was a strong female character, and that's what my mother wanted me to be. BINGO! Your wish came true, Mom!

Lesbian is the "L" in LGBTQ+. Raise your hand if you know where that term derives from. It's O.K. I can't see your hand. And if you played along, you're Lovely and Lively. Let's travel to the Northeastern Aegean Sea to find the third largest of the Greek Islands, Lesbos. Coordinates: 39°10′N26°20′E. GPS ready?

"The word *Lesbian* is derived from the name of the Greek island of Lesbos, home to the 6th-century BCE poet Sappho. From various ancient writings, historians gathered that a group of young women were left in Sappho's charge for their instruction or cultural edification. Little of Sappho's poetry survives, but her remaining poetry reflects the topics she wrote about: women's daily lives, their relationships, and rituals. She focused on the beauty of women and proclaimed her love for girls. Before the mid-19th century, the word *Lesbian* referred to any derivative or aspect of Lesbos, including a type of wine." (Wikipedia) Next in referring to Sappho as being in the sixth century with a reference later to the nineteenth century, without inserting the Before Christ or Before the Common Era, the antiquity of Sappho is lost. ~ Gale F. Stone, my friend and scholar.

Pop culture lesson? Check

Geography Lesson? Check

History Lesson? Check

Now, let's go into some modern political lessons. Let's start with a law called Title VII (that's a 7 in fancy Roman numerals!) of the Civil Rights Law of 1964. Stay with me, sometimes we must know our history so as to not repeat it.

Title VII of the Civil Rights Act of 1964 is a federal law that prohibits employers from discriminating against employees on the basis of sex, race, color, national origin, and religion. It generally applies to employers with 15 or more employees, including federal, state, and local governments. Title VII also applies to private and public colleges and universities, employment agencies, and labor organizations.

Both Title VII of the Civil Rights Act of 1964 and Title IX of the Education Amendments of 1972 provide protection against sex discrimination in the context of tenure. Title VII is a federal law that prohibits discrimination in employment on the basis of sex, as well as race, color, national origin, and religion. Title IX is a federal law that prohibits sex discrimination in education, covering all staff and students in any educational institution or program that receives federal funds. That's all great news, but does anyone notice anything missing?

Now take a look at the Movement Advancement Project by Googling "Equality Maps: State Nondiscrimination Laws." (2020). Find your state and see how your Legislation measures up for LGBTQ equality. You can also check out the Resources link on my website LisaKoenecke.com (under THE BOOK tab) for a link to the map.

Why is Wisconsin shown in light green with a gavel? According to the Wisconsin Department of Workforce Development, I can't be discriminated in hiring or firing for being gay...Hooray! Here's your human resource lesson for the day! If you are reading this and you don't live in Wisconsin, please check out your state in the aforementioned information.

Wisconsin Fair Employment Act Highlights

If you don't live in Wisconsin or another state that offers discrimination protections regarding sexual orientation, this information can form a great blueprint for creating change in your state.

"The Wisconsin Fair Employment Act prohibits employers, employment agencies, labor unions, licensing agencies, and other persons from discriminating against employees, job applicants, or licensing applicants because of their membership in specific protected categories, including sexual orientation.

"The Wisconsin Fair Employment Law defines "sexual orientation" as having a preference for heterosexuality, homosexuality, or bisexuality, having a history of such a preference, or being identified with such a preference.

"May an employer ask about an applicant's sexual orientation? The Fair Employment Law prohibits any inquiry that implies or expresses any limitation because of a protected basis, including sexual orientation. Marital status discrimination is also prohibited under Wisconsin law and questions about marital status that are designed to detect a person's sexual orientation may violate both marital status and sexual orientation provisions of the law.

"Is an individual protected if an employer thinks the employee's sexual orientation is different than it really is and acts on that perception?

Yes, the definition includes being identified with a preference for a particular sexual orientation. It is illegal for an employer to discriminate against someone based on perceived sexual orientation, even if the perception is wrong, for example, it would be a violation of the law if an employer assumes a man is homosexual because he is effeminate and discharges him because of that perception."

The Supreme Court heard three cases in 2019 that asked whether it is legal to fire workers because of their sexual orientation or gender identity (Title VII). That alone is enough to make those three of the most important employment discrimination cases in many years. But there are additional layers to these cases that could hurt all workers regardless of whether or not they are LGBTQ. Only 22 states prohibit employment discrimination based on sexual orientation and only 21 prohibit discrimination based on gender identity. So, if the Supreme Court rules in favor of the employers in *Zarda, Bostock, and Harris Funeral Homes,* millions of LGBTQ+ workers will be left without legal protections. Read on, my friend.

Let's see, Lisa was named after a soap opera and might lose protections because she's a lesbian? Looks like a little scary scenario to me and for my other LGBTQ+ friends. As my wife Angela, says, "Why do we need to legislate kindness and decency?" Makes you think, doesn't it?

How would you feel if you were fired for having brown eyes instead of blue? What if you lost your health benefits because you were left-handed? To paraphrase Lady Gaga, (because what self-respecting gay person wouldn't?) I was born this way. Who says Little Lisa from Loganville should be legislated against? Please show your rainbows, please stop homophobic jokes, and please vote! Lovely!

◆◆◆

"All of us who are openly gay are living and writing the history of our movement. We are no more—and no less—heroic than the suffragists and abolitionists of the 19th century; and the labor organizers, Freedom Riders, Stonewall demonstrators, and environmentalists of the 20th century. We are ordinary people, living our lives, and trying as civil-rights activist Dorothy Cotton said, to 'fix what ain't right' in our society." ~ Senator Tammy Baldwin

◆◆◆

"There will not be a magic day when we wake up and it's now okay to express ourselves publicly. We make that day by doing things publicly until it's simply the way things are." ~ Senator Tammy Baldwin

In 2013, Tammy Baldwin made history by becoming the first openly gay Senator in the United States. In her speech at the Millennium March for Equality, she spoke to LGBTQ folks, encouraging them to be out and proud. In this quotation, she states that the only way to normalize non-heterosexual orientations is for the queer community to act like they are normal, because they are.

M is for Microaggressions

Hello, friends and readers! Did you notice I didn't say ladies and gentlemen? In the LGBTQ+ world, greeting a group of people with "Ladies & Gentlemen" can be considered a microaggression. Yes, I know it's what we were taught to say, and now it's time to learn about being more inclusive!

As a former middle school counselor, it always bothered me when I would hear teachers greet a class by using "boys & girls." How about using the term "Scholars" or even "First hour?" (My close friend, Colleen Reilly, taught me that!) How about in the workplace? You could greet your audience with "Team," "Colleagues," or "Friends." Might I suggest you consider anything but "Ladies and Gentlemen?" What's your favorite non-binary greeting?

Let's learn more about microaggressions, shall we? According to Wikipedia, Microaggressions have been defined as *"brief and common daily verbal, behavioral, and environmental communications, whether intentional or unintentional, that transmit hostile, derogatory, or negative messages to a target person because they belong to a stigmatized group."*

Microaggressions are frequently unintentional. It doesn't have to be an outright insult or slur to hurt someone, and that's what makes microaggressions so complex. When my wife and I walk hand-in-hand, we often draw stares. That's a microaggression that over time makes us less likely to show this simple form of connection which heterosexuals take for granted.

Microaggressions often come out in the form of a stereotype, for example, expecting a gay man to be more stylish than other men, or expecting a lesbian to be stronger than other women. Consider these phrases in terms of microaggressions:

- You don't act gay.
- So, who's the man in the relationship? (I get this a lot!)
- I'm not being homophobic; you're just being too sensitive.
- You don't look trans.
- You're too pretty to be a lesbian.
- Have you ever had "real" sex?
- Since you're with a guy, you're a non-practicing bisexual, right?
- It's just a phase. You'll feel differently when you meet the right man/woman.

I have been called a man, or sir, more times than I can count. I used to let it go, but now, I will correct the person and remind them that girls can have short hair and dress in button-down shirts. After being labeled as male, the shock on their eyes when I turn

around is always the same because I can't pass as a male from the front! Some may call it gender non-conforming—which is coming up in the next chapter! —but I call it being my true self! Magnificent!

So, what do you do when you hear a microaggression? First, allow the person to whom the microaggression is directed to respond. If they seem unable to respond, pull out your capital "A" Ally hat and move from being a bystander to an Ally.

Oh, and when you aren't sure of a person's preferred gender, just call them Friend. Marvelous! M-kay?

◆◆◆

"When all Americans are treated as equal, no matter who they are or whom they love, we are all more free." ~ Barack Obama, 44th President of the United States of America

N is for Non-binary, Non-Conforming & Gender-Neutral Bathrooms

Welcome to the letter "N." Non-Binary and Non-Conforming are terms you might not have heard. Let's nudge our way into the nuances of these definitions...ha ha, alliteration never gets old! NEVER!

Gender binary is the classification of gender into two distinct, opposite, and disconnected forms of masculine and feminine, whether by social system or cultural belief. (Wikipedia, 2019) How many of you have ever gone through a drive-thru at a fast food restaurant? I loved taking my niece and nephew when they were younger. When we would order a meal that made us happy, the worker would ask if we wanted a toy for a "girl" or a "boy." A heavy sigh from Gauntie Lisa would follow every time as my non-binary radar was alerted. Can we just have a non-binary, non-conforming, gender-neutral toy?

If you remember, I was an early non-conformer when it came to stereotypical gender toys. My tractor and my G.I. Joe were my favorites. Why can't there just be toys that ALL kids can play with? And how about not making toys and clothes pink or blue? Boys can play with dolls and girls can play with trucks, right? Think twice before you buy that baby a gender-specific toy, please? Nifty!

Another truth about Lisa: I did NOT like wearing dresses or the color pink. Shocker? So, growing up in the 70s I was called a "tomboy." My favorite role model was Peppermint Patty and her sandals. Why did Marcie call her "sir?" There's a great article explaining how Schultz defied gender roles in creating Peppermint Patty, and yep— you guessed it!—you can find it in the Resources on my website at LisaKoenecke.com. I actually have a Peppermint Patty doll on my desk, next to my beaver bobble-head, and Franklin figurine from the Peanuts. Nice, right?

Non-binary is an umbrella term for a person who identifies with or expresses a gender identity that is neither entirely female nor entirely male. More from the Merriam Webster dictionary: *Gender identity refers to an individual's internalized psychological experience of being male or female, whereas gender nonconformity refers to the degree to which an individual's appearance, behavior, interests, and subjective self-concept deviate from conventional norms for masculinity/femininity.* ~ Lisa M. Diamond, Susan B. Bonner, and Janna Dickenson

When I wear a tuxedo to a formal event, I am an example of gender non-conforming. The older I get, the less I enjoy wearing "left-handed" zippered trousers. Most of the world would know them as "women's" trousers. I prefer to wear dress pants that I get at a thrift store in the men's section. We even have a gender non-conforming puppy.

Madi identifies as female (we asked her) and yet, when she goes tinkle she raises her little girl leg like boy puppies do. I am SO Proud! During my time as a middle school counselor, I had one student who identified as gender-fluid: a mix of both genders, who may feel more male on some days and more female on others. I would greet the student at the door in the morning to determine their identity for the day. I would say, "Good morning, _____?" and wait for the student to show me a 1 for male, and a 2 for female for the day. I would then send out an email to the student's teachers sharing the student's preferred gender/name for the day. It made such a huge difference in creating a supportive environment for that student!

Gender-Neutral Bathrooms (All Gender Restrooms)

If you grew up in a home with people of different genders in the same space, chances are you experienced a gender-neutral bathroom starting at a very young age. My wife grew up in a household with 6 people sharing one bathroom, including 3 females and 3 males. It was every person for themselves when nature called! A gender-neutral bathroom simply means that it is not labeled specifically for use by women only or men only. You may see them referred to as "unisex," "family," or "all gender." I prefer the term "all gender" due to its inclusive nature.

All gender bathrooms make sense to me. Think about going to a concert or an event in a big stadium. How long are the lines to the women's restrooms compared to the men's? If you haven't noticed the lines, you probably haven't stood in the LONG line. Maybe we need more porta potties? Everything anyone needs in one space!

Going back to sharing a bathroom with family members of other genders, you still were able to have space to yourself to take care of personal matters, right? All Gender bathrooms are the same way. It's common for more progressive public spaces to have single rooms with a lock for the toilet area with a common area for handwashing and mirrors. Yep! All Gender and very private!

It can be intimidating and downright scary for someone who is gender non-conforming to use a bathroom that doesn't appear to be aligned with their outward appearance. Schools are starting to understand this reality. People can be very aggressive verbally and even physically when someone who is gender non-conforming uses "their" restroom. Why not make everyone safer by creating safe spaces for everyone?

As more people become comfortable with their identities, we will see the need for more inclusivity in the workplace. It used to be that middle school students would start by saying they were bisexual if they were not sure of their identity. Then the term questioning/queer came along. Queer is still here, most often used in genderqueer. Now, I believe more and more young people will identify as trans in the near future. As more and more famous people come "out" as trans, we will see more teens identifying as non-binary and non-conforming. Because of this, gender-neutral bathrooms will become even more critical in the coming years.

Last, but not least, I predict we'll start to see more people using the courtesy title of Mx. Rather than the traditional Mr., Mrs., Miss, or the title of Ms. which became popular in 1986, Mx. is becoming more accepted as a gender-neutral option. Check out the article from USA Today on using Mx as a formal title. Where? The Resources link on my website LisaKoenecke.com (under THE BOOK tab).

As Rachel Maddow would say, "Watch this space." I sure hope to meet her one day!

◆◆◆

"I think being gay is a blessing, and it's something I am thankful for every single day."
~ Anderson Cooper, journalist

O is for Out

As a disclaimer, everyone Owns their Own coming Out story. It is never O.K. to out someone. It is their story alone to share, if they want to, and when THEY are ready. If you want to know if someone is gay, ask them directly in a safe and respectful manner. If someone asks you if another person is gay, please tell them to ask that person. If someone comes out to you, please say "Thank You." That's the best validation we can receive. I will give you a glimpse into my coming out story.

In the LGBTQ world, we are born this way (just ask Lady Gaga), yet some of us stay in the closet for safety and to not be Ostracized. Coming Out is a process, not just a one-time event. The privilege I have includes the color of my white skin, my socio-economic status, and my middle-class upbringing. I don't HAVE to come Out to people. You can't see gay like you can see skin color or ability, unless, of course, your gaydar is perfectly tuned, meaning you can tell someone is gay by looking at them. When you look at me, your gaydar probably goes off, and I am O.K. with that! Oye, you bet I'm Out and not in the closet.

From the Urban dictionary, "in the closet" is a term used to describe "a homosexual person who has not told anyone of their sexual orientation." As you read earlier, I was in the closet until my sister told me I was gay. It was Thanksgiving 1996 and I was 27 years old. Kind of a late bloomer—I know, I know! During dinner I was complaining that I couldn't find any boys I wanted to date. My sister replied, "That's because you're gay. Please pass the carrots." I started crying. It actually made a lot of sense after I stopped to think about it. The end. Well, not really. It was just the beginning of my coming out story and journey, and I still like carrots!

National Coming OUT Day

October 11th every year is National Coming OUT Day. Please mark your calendars. In fact, every year I remind school counselors to be ready for middle and high schoolers coming out to them on October 11th. Thank you to all of you for being a safe person!

The Human Rights Campaign offers free resource guides on the following topics to help answer your questions about supporting those who come Out, including some resources in Spanish:

Coming OUT as your true identity	Workplace
Family & Community	Healthcare
Youth Resources & Reports	Recursos para "salir del closet"
Religion & Faith	

National Coming OUT Day is a significant observance for the LGBTQ+ community as well as for our families, our allies, and our communities. On Oct. 11, 1987, half a million people participated in the March on Washington for Lesbian and Gay Rights. Thank you to the Human Rights Campaign for their advocacy around this rite of passage for some, or perhaps a day of deep reflection and consideration for those fearing their own coming out.

The other thing to consider is that while coming out may have a single day of celebration, for many of us, coming out can be a daily consideration. Every time someone who identifies as LGBTQ+ meets a new person, the person identifying as LGBTQ+ has to make a decision whether to reveal their true identity. Is it worth the risk? I can tell you it's mentally exhausting.

Think about the last time you listened to a presenter or a trainer or a professional speaker. Consider that most heterosexual speakers and authors will include their spouse in their bio. They may include their spouse in their introduction or talk about their spouse from the stage without giving it another thought. Believe me that LGBTQ+ speakers ALWAYS think about it before coming out. In fact, I am worried about getting hate mail or even being shunned and not getting hired to speak because I'm gay. This is why I am the Inclusion Ally and not the LGBTQ+ Expert. I just want to be your Everyday Gay, O.K?

For a long time, I wasn't out to my students as a middle school counselor. After having a 7th grade student tell me it was easier pretending to be a boy than it was to be gay in the small town we were in, I realized I needed to do something differently. The difficult part for me was being afraid of losing my job because I was gay, and officially being out to the school community was a huge risk. I was also a girls' basketball coach and refused to ever go into their locker room so I wouldn't get accused of anything creepy. Consider how many coaches use those final locker room moments to pump up their team. Yet I felt I couldn't. I wanted people to respect me as a school counselor...who just happened to be gay. Every time I started in a new school district, I had to do my research to see if they were open and affirming of my lifestyle. This was Not always fun! Enumeration matters!

I am happy to say that I am now out and proud, which isn't to say that everyone I meet knows I'm gay. To put people at ease so they don't have to guess or even ask, I will frequently mention my wife, Angela and use our female pronouns. I can tell in seconds whether or not we will be accepted. The stress of coming out can be too much to bear for some people. My goal with this book is to save lives by offering resources to support our LGBTQ+ population, our families and our allies. I continue to work to share my experiences to create a better world for all of the people who are not yet out, or those who have been ostracized when they have taken the risk to come out.

A gentle, yet firm, reminder: NEVER, NEVER OUT anyone else. It's their story to tell. If someone asks you if someone is gay, bisexual, transgender, etc., tell that person to ask the source. Even if you know, it is not your story to tell. When someone comes out to you, please remember to say, "Thank you!" YOU are a safe person, and someone will come out to you if they haven't already!

◆◆◆

"I believe that no one should ever have to choose between a career we love and living our lives with authenticity and integrity" ~ Selisse Berry, Out & Equal Founding Executive Director

P is for Pride & PFLAG

Let's chat about why the term Pride is so important to us, and why Parents and Friends of Lesbians And Gays (PFLAG) is such an amazing resource, especially in Wisconsin! PRIDE is an LGBTQ+ term of solidarity. In June, it's common to greet each other with "Happy Pride!" It's kind of like wishing someone a fabulous "Good Morning." Let's start with a history of PRIDE. Feel free to go back to the Fun with Flags chapter for visuals.

On June 28, 1969 in Greenwich, New York, police raided the Stonewall Inn. The Stonewall Riots Anniversary is June 28, 1969. This is a day to remember the Stonewall Riots which are described as the start of the Trans and Gay Liberation Movement in the United States. It's a day for people to remember the biracial lesbian and drag king Stormé DeLarverie whose scuffle with the police started the rebellion. That's why we celebrate our PRIDE the entire month of June. When people ask when is straight pride month? I tell them, whenever you want it, that it is your privilege to not have to declare a month. Sorry to be snarky, but it's true. Just like you don't need a straight flag to represent your majority. It just is.

According to Wikipedia, "*Gay pride or LGBT pride* is the promotion of the self-affirmation, dignity, equality, and increased visibility of lesbian, gay, bisexual, and transgender (LGBT) people as a social group. *Pride,* as opposed to shame and social stigma, is the predominant outlook that bolsters most LGBT rights movements."

Unfortunately, the rise of social media has spawned an increase of hate-filled attacks on virtually every marginalized group. It can be tempting as an LGBTQ+ individual to live a life hidden in the shadows, not sharing who we are and who we love for fear of the types of social media attacks that are rampant across the Internet. This is my reality publishing this book. Will there be hate mail, hateful comments, or even threats? I hope not. Again, I have to be strong, dear reader, and blaze a trail for those who follow in my rainbow footprints. Thanks again for being my Ally!

Pride plays an important role in sharing ALL of who we are as individuals. Pride to me means greeting my wife at the airport with all the affection and love that a straight couple shows. It means coming out to my graduate students at the beginning of each semester without fear of losing my job for being gay at a private UCC university. And it means being accepted by everyone—family and strangers alike. Unfortunately, not everyone agrees that I, and all LGBTQ+ people, should have these rights. Luckily, we have allies like you advocating alongside us every day. We can choose our family when we are old enough, or reach out to PFLAG for support. Did you know that PFLAG serves ALL identities, not just lesbians and gays?

PFLAG

As of 2020, PFLAG has 500 chapters and more than 200,000 national members. The idea for PFLAG began in 1972 when Jeanne Manford marched with her son, Morty, in New York's Christopher Street Liberation Day March, the precursor to today's Pride parade. She urged parents to unite in support of their gay children. My mom, Marlene would have been Jeanne's best friend! Probably!

PFLAG lives its three part-mission: First and foremost, to support parents and families of lesbians, gays, transgender, and bisexuals who are having problems accepting their relative's sexual orientation. Additionally, they support the spouses of newly out LGBTQ people. Secondly, they strive to educate themselves and others about LGBTQ issues. Thirdly, they are visible advocates for issues affecting the LGBTQ family, such as discrimination in the workplace and housing. They work for equality for all LGBTQ civil rights.

If you live in the Madison, Wisconsin, area and if you visit the Dane County Farmer's Market on a Saturday during the summer, please thank the volunteers from PFLAG for their advocacy. If you don't live in the Madison area, please spread the word about PFLAG and the Positive work they Provide! Reach out to them for yourself or a friend that needs their support—or to expand your allyship even further!

◆◆◆

"I'm not missing a minute of this. It's the revolution!" ~ Sylvia Rivera, activist

This is one of the most famous quotes to come out of the Stonewall Riots. Uttered by Latina LGBTQ activist Sylvia Rivera, this statement served as a rallying cry for many who were afraid of the violence that occurred at Stonewall. Rivera knew the dangers, but also knew that the risk was worth the potential reward. She knew that the queer community had been put down for long enough and was ready to fight for their rights and for their voice. Participating in the riots at only 17 years old, Rivera was an inspiration to many.

Q is for Queer

Hey Lisa! Isn't the term *Queer* offensive? Why are you writing about that word? Thanks for asking, dear reader. I will give you a Quick history of the term Queer later in this chapter. Questioning is another term we use for the "Q" in our acronym LGBTQ. Questioning was used early on by middle schoolers in my school counseling career, but today, I hear more students identifying as genderqueer or transgender, skipping right over Questioning. Quaint!

I would be curious to see what your reaction was when you saw this title. Some will want to read and learn; others will quietly quake over this chapter. Thank you for those of you still reading— you are my people!

Miriam Webster defines *"Queer: of, relating to, or characterized by sexual or romantic attraction that is not limited to people of a particular gender identity or sexual orientation."* My generation (X) doesn't use Queer as much as the generations following mine (Generation Y/Millennial, and Gen Z) use it.

Perhaps this will bring a smile to your face. Have you seen the cable show "Queer Eye?" *"Queer Eye is an American reality television series that premiered on the cable television network Bravo in July 2003. Originally* Queer Eye for the Straight Guy, *the title was later shortened to broaden the overall scope"* (Wikipedia). What I love about the show is how the Fab Five, as the main cast are known, help others. It's not about the Queer lifestyle or focused on Queer relationships. It's about paying it forward. Who is your favorite character? Original cast or latest cast?

I promised you more on the history of the term *Queer*. Historically, *queer* meant not straight. If you have ever ridden in a car with me, I use the term *gaily* forward rather than straight when it comes to directions. *"By the early 1900s, "queer" became used to reference homosexuals both by people within the community (Gertrude Stein in her poetry, for example) and people outside of the community (newspapers, for instance),"* Marissa Higgins writes in an article for *Bustle*.com. In the 1950s, the term queer held a negative connotation like dyke (*having to do with a water tool, it's actually spelled dike, not dyke which is another term for a lesbian*) or faggot (*a bundle of sticks or a british cigarette*). Enter the 1980s and the LGBTQ+ world worked to reclaim the word and offer it as a more inclusive umbrella term for our population. Higgins writes, *"A word like "queer" encompasses sexual orientation, gender identity, and gender expression concisely."*

So, is it o.k. for anyone to use the term *Queer*? I would ask each individual how they identify. If they use the term to identify themselves, then you can probably use it when talking with them. If they don't use it, you don't use it. Questions? There won't be a Quiz, I just had to use as many "Q" words as was Quantifiable.

Quite lovely of you for reading.

◆◆◆

"The only queer people are those who don't love anybody." ~ Rita Mae Brown, author

◆◆◆

"If homosexuality is a disease, let's all call in queer to work: 'Hello. Can't work today, still queer.'" ~ Robin Tyler, activist and main stage producer for the 1979, 1987, and 1993 Marches on Washington for Lesbian and Gay Rights

R is for Riddle Scale (No joke!)

You haven't heard of the Riddle Scale? No worries, not everyone has, let's Relax, Rewind, and Review...see what I did there? I crack myself up! Even though this isn't a riddle. Ha ha!

Remember, I like to start with a definition, so here ya go: *"The Riddle scale is a psychometric scale that measures the degree to which a person is or is not homophobic. The scale was frequently used in tolerance education about anti-discriminatory attitudes regarding sexual orientation. It is named after its creator, psychologist Dorothy Riddle."* (Wikipedia 2019)

Who was Dorothy Riddle? Thanks for asking! During the early 1970s, she was part of an American Psychological Association Task Force which was ultimately responsible for the official change in the status of homosexuality from a psychiatric disorder to a lifestyle. As mentioned previously, she also developed the Riddle Scale, a tool for measuring homophobia that is now being used to measure changes in a range of other social attitudes.

The Riddle Scale

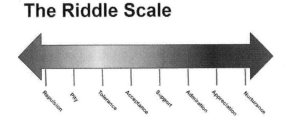

Isn't it sad that attitudes have to be measured by levels? Growing up, did your parents have "the talk" with you about being repulsed or nurtured? Mine sure didn't with me. When a baby is born, the dreams are of course to have a happy and healthy baby. I know that my mom had dreams of me getting married (to a man), giving her grandbabies, and probably to not be repulsed by it all.

Let's review the Riddle Scale from Wikipedia:

1. **Repulsion**: Homosexuality is seen as a crime against nature. Gays/lesbians are considered sick, crazy, immoral, sinful, wicked, etc. Anything is justified to change them: incarceration, hospitalization, behavior therapy, electroconvulsive therapy, etc.
2. **Pity**: Represents heterosexual chauvinism. Heterosexuality is considered more mature and certainly to be preferred. It is believed that any possibility

of becoming straight should be reinforced, and those who seem to be born that way should be pitied as less fortunate ("the poor dears").

3. **Tolerance**: Homosexuality is viewed as a phase of adolescent development that many people go through and most people grow out of. Thus, lesbians/gays are less mature than straights and should be treated with the protectiveness and indulgence one uses with children who are still maturing. It is believed that lesbians/gays should not be given positions of authority because they are still working through their adolescent behavior.

4. **Acceptance**: Still implies that there is something to accept; the existing climate of discrimination is ignored. Characterized by such statements as "You're not lesbian to me, you're a person!" or "What you do in bed is your own business," or "That's fine with me as long as you don't flaunt it!"

5. **Support**: People at this level may be uncomfortable themselves, but they are aware of the homophobic climate and the irrational unfairness, and work to safeguard the rights of lesbians and gays.

6. **Admiration**: It is acknowledged that being lesbian/gay in our society takes strength. People at this level are willing to truly examine their homophobic attitudes, values, and behaviors.

7. **Appreciation**: The diversity of people is considered valuable and lesbians/gays are seen as a valid part of that diversity. People on this level are willing to combat homophobia in themselves and others.

8. **Nurturance**: Assumes that gay/lesbian people are indispensable in our society. People on this level view lesbians/gays with genuine affection and delight, and are willing to be their allies and advocates.

To provide some context, at my first wedding (to a woman), my mom was there because my aunts and uncles were the best and ensured she would be there. I had written a letter to my father asking him to bring my mother, but, to no avail. I didn't invite my brother because of his attitude toward me. My father didn't show up.

So, let's do the math on my immediate family: Father = Repulsed (1), Brother = Repulsed (1), Sister = Tolerated (3) but didn't show up, and Mother = Supported (5). As you can see, no Admiration (6), no Appreciation (7), no Nurturance (8). I don't tell you this to feel sorry for me, but rather to explain why I advocate for those lower on the Riddle Scale. My aunts and uncles admired, appreciated and have always nurtured me.

In addition to my aunts and uncles, I get my admiration, appreciation, and nurturance from my "chosen family" composed of friends. Have you heard of Friendsgiving? Let's strive to support, admire, appreciate, and ultimately nurture, shall we? That would be a great goal as an Ally! I nurture and recognize you! Really!

Hmm...50 years ago, as I was growing up in the 1970s, I was considered to have a psychiatric disorder. Now I can hope for a Level (4) Acceptance. It does get better! Really! Keep in mind that although 'tolerance' and 'acceptance' can be seen as positive attitudes, they should actually be treated as negative because they can mask underlying fear or hatred (Really, who would be o.k. with only being tolerated?).

Throughout my career, one of my favorite resources for social justice and equitable education has been Teaching Tolerance. Teaching Tolerance (Tolerance = Level 3 for those of you playing at home) is based out of Atlanta as part of the Southern Poverty Law Center, and was founded in 1991 to prevent the growth of hate. Here is a quote from their website: *"Tolerance is surely an imperfect term, yet the English language offers no single word that embraces the broad range of skills we need to live together peacefully."*

For my Wisconsin friends (really all of you, but the story was based in Wisconsin), Teaching Tolerance has a free DVD resource called *"Bullied."* It is based upon the true story of Jaime Nabozny growing up in Ashland, Wisconsin. Jamie was severely bullied in middle and high school and the district did nothing to protect him. He sued the Ashland School District in 1996 and a jury awarded him $962,000 in damages. Right in my backyard...WOW! This case made national headlines and was a catalyst for new anti-LGBTQ bullying laws.

In addition to Showing you're an Ally, Shifting mindsets and behaviors, and Shaping your environment to be inclusive, your goals as an Ally should include:

- Striving for Level 8 and Nurturing EVERYONE, especially if they are LGBTQ+
- Checking out the free resources and/or subscribing to the free magazine from Teaching Tolerance.

◆◆◆

"We need, in every community, a group of angelic troublemakers." ~ Bayard Rustin, activist

If you aren't familiar with the name "Bayard Rustin," you may recognize one of his closest associates: Martin Luther King Jr. Rustin was an important figure in the Civil Rights Movement, fighting not only for the rights of African Americans, but for the LGBTQ community as well. Rustin urged the disenfranchised to engage in civil disobedience to get their points across to the majority, encouraging those who wanted to fight for their rights to be unafraid to speak up and act out to demand them.

S is for Show, Shift, Shape

Show, Shift, and Shape are the three words I used to support my TEDx talk *"Allies Save Lives"* on February 13th, 2020. Shameless plug! Sorry—not Sorry!

Soooooooo, here are three ways you can become a Super Ally. Allies Save Lives by Showing you are an ally.

SHOW you are an ally by wearing a rainbow ribbon, displaying a rainbow sticker or exhibit your allyship with a rainbow pin. Why is a rainbow so important? A rainbow symbolizes safety, family and hope to those of us in the LGBTQ population. (Check out the chapter on Fun with Flags to learn more.)

SHIFTING mindsets and perceptions is a second way to SHOW you are an Ally. Let's revisit what it means to be an ally. Deep in my heart, I want to believe that almost everyone is an ally and has a desire to learn more in order to support our community even further than they are currently. When ally is spelled starting with a small "a," it states you are someone who could be an associate, a friend, or a colleague. A small "a" ally might hear a homophobic joke, and, even though deep in their soul it's not a nice joke, a small "a" ally might not say anything. What if we were to SHIFT that small "a" ally to a capital "A" Ally? Let's take that homophobic joke example and see what an "A" Ally would do. Shift to the next paragraph.

SHIFTING mindsets and behaviors, a capital "A" Ally will say something about the homophobic joke. A capital "A" Ally might say, "not cool" or "knock it off" to the person telling the hurtful joke. When others witness this, their mindsets, and perceptions SHIFT as well. My hope is that SHIFT will help us in SHAPING inclusive policies and procedures.

SHAPING policies and procedures is not always a simple stint (had to use an "s" there). Seeing yourself specifically enumerated as an under-represented population or listed as a minority group in policies is something I find extremely important. When I was searching for a school counseling position, I looked at each district's policies to see if sexual orientation was listed as a protected class and if they had any policies protecting students not identifying with the mainstream culture. I continue to use this technique in my daily life regarding interacting with businesses—determining where I spend my money, volunteer my time, and share my talents.

In my TEDx talk *"Allies Save Lives,"* I share the SHIFT brought about in my own life by a seventh-grade student. Because of events experienced by that student and another family in our district, we were able to advocate for more inclusive policies regarding pupil non-discrimination. I certainly could not have done it solo. We became the Seventh (can't make that "s" up) district in the State of Wisconsin to have such inclusive policies. It was a big win! Score!

You are truly an ally because of your interest in educating yourself further by reading this book. Dare I say you are also an Ally? Thank you for continuing to SHOW your allyship. Thank you for continuing to SHIFT mindsets and perceptions, so that we can start SHAPING some new policies and procedures for the LGBTQ community.

◆◆◆

"It takes some intelligence and insight to figure out you're gay and then a tremendous amount of balls to live it and live it proudly." ~ Jason Bateman, actor, director, and producer

◆◆◆

"Every gay and lesbian person who has been lucky enough to survive the turmoil of growing up is a survivor. Survivors always have an obligation to those who will face the same challenges." ~ Bob Paris, writer and actor

T is for Transgender & the Trevor Project

Top of Mind for the letter "T" is the word of Transgender. As a reminder, we say *Transgender* not *Transgendered*.

Our world is lucky to have more and more people becoming their true selves and identifying as they truly are. Ten years ago, I only had two students who were identifying as Transgender in a building of 800 students. Today, there are many many more resources and even role models out there. Terrific!

There is a difference between Transgender and Transsexual. Remember the cult classic movie *Rocky Horror Picture Show*? I'll be giving you some more updated information, but if you haven't seen the movie, see it! I loved it. Toast! Another great video to watch is *9 Biggest Transgender Celebrities* (as of 2020). Consider this vocabulary from Dictionary.com to help level our collective play fields:

- **"Transgender**: adjective; denoting or relating to a person whose sense of personal identity and gender does not correspond with their birth sex.
- **"Transitioning**: verb; to change from one gender identity to another or to align one's dress, behavior, etc., with one's gender identity.
- **"Transvestite**: noun; a person, typically a man, who derives pleasure from dressing in clothes primarily associated with the opposite sex.
- **"Transsexual**: noun; a person who emotionally and psychologically feels that they belong to the opposite sex."

Please remember, this is just a tiny start. For Frequently Asked Questions please go to The National Center for Transgender Equality. The National Center for Transgender Equality was founded in 2003 by transgender activists who recognized the urgent need for policy change to advance transgender equality. With a committed board of directors, a volunteer staff of one, and donated office space, they set out to accomplish what no one had yet done: provide a powerful transgender advocacy presence in Washington, D.C.

Today, NCTE has grown to a staff of over 20 and works at the local, state, and federal levels to change laws, policies, and society.

Check out the complete list of FAQs from The National Center for Transgender Equality's website. They do a much better job of explaining than I ever could. My takeaways from their amazing site:

1. Don't ask anyone about their junk...EVER! (Would you want to answer questions about yours? I didn't think so!)

2. You can use the term "Trans."

3. If you mess up with pronouns or other misunderstandings on your own part, own the mistake, apologize, and ask how to make it better for that person moving forward.

4. Conversion Therapy doesn't work...trust me! I have my Master's in Counseling!

5. We don't get to say how someone identifies. Let them live THEIR life!

6. More people will be using Mx. as their formal title in their name. For example, you may see a roster including Miss Black, Ms. White, and Mx. Green. Refer back to Gender Non-conforming in chapter N for more information.

Transitioning to another Terrific and Talented resource, the Trevor Project.

The Trevor Project is the world's largest suicide prevention and crisis intervention organization for LGBTQ (lesbian, gay, bisexual, transgender, queer, and questioning) young people. The organization works to save young lives by providing support through free and confidential suicide prevention and crisis intervention programs on platforms where young people spend their time: 24/7 phone lifeline, chat, and text. I mention the Trevor Project in my TEDx talk, *"Allies Save Lives"* and I try to tell as many people as I can about this FREE lifesaving resource.

◆◆◆

"If a transvestite doesn't say I'm gay and I'm proud and I'm a transvestite, then nobody else is going to hop up there and say I'm gay and I'm proud and I'm a transvestite for them."~ Marsha P. Johnson, activist and self-identified drag queen

Another important figure in the Stonewall Riots, Marsha P. Johnson was also one of the first activists to fight for the rights and dignity of drag queens. She was vocal throughout her life about the unique struggles faced by those who dressed in drag and encouraged others not to become complacent and to continue fighting for rights and respect.

◆◆◆

"Nature made a mistake, which I have corrected." ~ Christine Jorgensen, activist

Christine Jorgensen was one of the first people to undergo sex reassignment surgery, and the first to publicly speak about the process. While many decried her decision as unnatural, she made the bold assertion that nature was wrong in putting her into a man's body, and that the reassignment surgery made things right. Her advocacy aimed to normalize transgenderism and allow those who identified as trans to understand and accept themselves for who they truly are.

◆◆◆

"I've been embraced by a new community. That's what happens when you're finally honest about who you are; you find others like you." ~ Chaz Bono, writer, musician, actor

U is for UUA and UCC

Ugg, that's a lot of "U"s I'm using! Ultimately, alliteration cracks me up every time! If you read this title and thought I would be talking about some youth sports leagues or some type of ultimate fighting, nope! This chapter is about open and affirming faith institutions. Yes, I know these are two Christian examples, and I know there are many more out there. Please don't be upset if I didn't mention your spiritual family.

If you remember my religious journey, it started in Loganville (a suburb of Reedsburg), Wisconsin, on top of a hill. If you don't remember my journey...buckle up! Here we go! In the Unincorporated township of Loganville (I grew up on a farm), there were two Lutheran churches. St. Peter's was Wisconsin Synod Lutheran, and this was where the rich farmers went (They had snacks during Sunday School). We went to St. John's Missouri Synod Lutheran on top of the hill (Not the rich farmers = no snacks. Hey! It was a big deal for a kid!). I wanted to be a minister. Yep! True story! Mainly because I LOVED talking from the pulpit. Then I found out that the Missouri Synod did not value women. Women/girls could not serve in any office, or be an usher, or ANYTHING. UGGH! Talk about not feeling included! Unnecessary if you ask me. Ultimate girl power!

I consider myself more of a spiritual person than a religious one, but I can appreciate those religions who tend to be welcoming to the LGBTQ community. Enter, the Unitarian Universalist Association and the United Church of Christ. First, a bit about the Unitarian Universalist Association from their website.

"The UUA is the central organization for the Unitarian Universalist (UU) religious movement in the United States. The UUA's 1,000+ member congregations are committed to Seven Principles that include the worth of each person, the need for justice and compassion, and the right to choose one's own beliefs according to uua.org. As UU Rev. Barbara Wells ten Hove explains, 'The Principles are not dogma or doctrine, but rather a guide for those of us who choose to join and participate in Unitarian Universalist religious communities.'"

1. *1st Principle*: The inherent worth and dignity of every person;
2. *2nd Principle*: Justice, equity, and compassion in human relations;
3. *3rd Principle*: Acceptance of one another and encouragement to spiritual growth in our congregations;
4. *4th Principle*: A free and responsible search for truth and meaning;
5. *5th Principle*: The right of conscience and the use of the democratic process within our congregations and in society at large;

6. *6th Principle*: The goal of world community with peace, liberty, and justice for all;

7. *7th Principle:* Respect for the interdependent web of all existence of which we are a part.

I kind of dig the idea of the UUA world valuing the inherent worth of EACH person! In fact, it was in a UUA building that I first met my wife. My friend and boss at the time, Jeanne Sears, was marrying her wife, Becky Burns. I was a friend of the bride, Jeanne, and Angela was a friend of the bride, Becky. That's a story to tell over an adult beverage. Let me buy you a beverage and I'll share! Then, I'll tell you about the Miss Reedsburg parade candy-throwing event! If you know me well, you know that story!

Back to the UUA story. Did you know that they have rainbows in their logos and messaging? Yep! We in the LGBTQ+ world know that you are an open and affirming (safe) person, place, or community of faith when we see the rainbow flag in your signage, on your buildings, or in your logos. Thank you, UUA!

That takes us to the UCC or the United Church of Christ. Please understand, I am not recommending one or the other. I am not even recommending you become religious, I am just offering more ABCs of the LGBTQ+ world. This chapter is a resource for you to consider how other organizations, associations, and businesses can be more inclusive to the LGBTQ+ world as well as how to best show they are welcoming to the outside world.

Directly from the United Church of Christ's website UCC.org, here is what they believe:

- "We believe that each person is unique and valuable. It is the will of God that every person belongs to a family of faith where they have a strong sense of being valued and loved.
- We believe that each person is on a spiritual journey and that each of us is at a different stage of that journey.
- We believe that the persistent search for God produces an authentic relationship with God, engendering love, strengthening faith, dissolving guilt, and giving life purpose and direction."

Uff da! I used to work in a primarily Scandinavian community and picked up this common exclamation of surprise. You're welcome! That was a lot of religious talk for a non-religious book. Take what you like; leave what you don't. No worries here. There are lots of options out there regarding faith and even spiritualism. I just really want to remind you, dear reader, about the power of the rainbow and what it symbolizes to our community. And just how easy it is to show that you are welcoming to all.

The UCC uses the Bible verse John 17:21 "That all may be one," which happens to be the verse I used at YMCA Camp Edwards. Super cool how my worlds come together. I am also proudly working at Lakeland University which is based upon the UCC beliefs. One day, I'll change their mission statement from including the phrase "men and women" to the word "individuals." Always working to shift policies! I'll keep you posted on that journey in my blog.

◆◆◆

"So, let me be clear: I'm proud to be gay, and I consider being gay among the greatest gifts God has given me." ~ Tim Cook, CEO, Apple, Inc.

◆◆◆

"It is against this God who kills that we are fighting and resisting." ~ Alexya Salvador

Organized religion has been one of the harshest critics of homosexuality, citing holy writings as evidence that it goes against God. Alexya Salvador, set to become the first transgender pastor in Brazil, doesn't necessarily see religion as the enemy of LGBTQ rights. As she states in this quotation, it is a particular version of God, one that is vengeful and judgmental, that must be eradicated. She strives for a different view of God: one that is accepting and loving of everyone, regardless of their identities. She hopes to usher in a new era of love and understanding between religion and the LGBTQ community.

◆◆◆

"The Lord is my Shepherd and he knows I'm gay." ~ Troy Perry

Troy Perry founded the Metropolitan Community Church: A Protestant denomination that specializes in welcoming the LGBTQ community. Perry was religious for much of his life, but was frustrated by feeling unwelcome as a gay man. With his ministry, he strives to give others a place of love, welcoming, and acceptance. He is also a vocal advocate encouraging other faith communities to open their doors to the queer community.

V is for Volunteering

In advocating for the LGBTQ+ community, one of the most rewarding ways to spend my time is Volunteering. This chapter is dedicated to both the organizations that thrive through volunteerism, and to you, dear reader, as you discover new opportunities to expand your impact as an Ally through volunteering. Please note that I'm providing a handful of resources and ideas where you, too, can volunteer. Please share your favorite LGBTQ+ organizations where you volunteer as well. Comments are always welcomed on my blog. Or if you're reading this in the future, I will probably have a cool new communication system not even invented in 2020.

We are extremely lucky to live in the Madison, Wisconsin, area. Our favorite organization to volunteer for is GSAFE: The Gay Straight Alliance for Safe Schools. GSAFE is where I became the Lunch Lady and "Lady Rainbow." For many years I volunteered in the kitchen during GSAFE's Leadership Development Institute, an immersive program that helped student activists more deeply understand their rights in school and to find their voices to speak out. (Cool, right?) I'd prepare and serve meals with 1-2 other volunteers for up to 100 student leaders per event. In case you're wondering, Sloppy Joes or Sloppy Josephines were not on our menu. We just called them Sloppy Sandwiches. Vegetarian, Vegan and any other dietary identities were honored and respected.

Each Fall, a popular GSAFE fundraiser was their Run/Walk/Eat. (Hooray! Food!) Each year, I dress in rainbow attire from head to toe and lead the registration team for participants and the dozens of volunteers required to put on an event of this magnitude. I'd also use my old camp director voice to gather people and give directions to the start of the race. Good times! And a fun use of my not-so-shy personality! Hence, Lady Rainbow! Viola!

My wife volunteered on the GSAFE board of directors for three years, as well as for other events and fundraisers—you could say we're a GSAFE family! When I would get questions regarding LGBTQ+ issues that I couldn't answer, I would rattle off their phone number (608) 661-4141 and website www.gsafewi.org as THE venue for resources.

If you happen to live outside of Wisconsin, I invite you to look into another of my favorite LGBTQ+ organizations offering virtual volunteer opportunities: GLSEN. GLSEN is the Gay Lesbian Straight Education Network. They celebrate a Day of Silence in schools each year, among providing other projects and resources. Yes, I did talk about them in the "G" chapter. Well done, dear reader. Let's do a deep dive into the Day of Silence again. You're welcome!

The GLSEN Day of Silence is a national, student-led demonstration where LGBTQ students and allies all around the country—and the world—take a vow of silence to protest the harmful effects of harassment and discrimination of LGBTQ people in schools. Started in the mid-90s by two college students, the Day of Silence has expanded to reach hundreds of thousands of students each year. Every April, students go through the school day without speaking; ending the day with Breaking the Silence rallies and events to share their experiences during the protest and bringing attention to ways their schools and communities can become more inclusive.

In 2020 GLSEN honored the 25th anniversary of Day of Silence.

Another great organization with tremendous volunteers is PFLAG: Parents & Friends of Lesbians and Gays. Please remember that PFLAG serves more than lesbians and gays. There are over 400 chapters of PFLAG in the United States to help families and friends with resources and ways to volunteer. In Madison, we have a wonderful farmer's market every Saturday morning. Each time we walk by the PFLAG table—which is always staffed with fabulous volunteers—we thank them for being there and for volunteering! Yep, more repetition. Remember, you need to have seven encounters with something for it to stick in your brain.

In previous chapters, you've learned about the Trevor Project and the Human Rights Campaign (HRC). There are hundreds of organizations around the country to investigate, depending on your area of expertise and interest. A few more to check into:

- **GLAAD** (Gay & Lesbian Alliance Against Defamation) rewrites the script for LGBTQ acceptance. As a dynamic media force, GLAAD tackles tough issues to shape the narrative and provoke dialogue that leads to cultural change. GLAAD protects all that has been accomplished and creates a world where everyone can live the life they love.

- **COLAGE** (Children of Lesbians and Gays Everywhere) is a national movement of children, youth, and adults with one or more lesbian, gay, bisexual, transgender and/or queer (LGBTQ) parent/s. COLAGE builds community and works toward social justice through youth empowerment, leadership development, education, and advocacy.

- **It Gets Better Project**: The It Gets Better Project is a nonprofit organization with a mission to uplift, empower, and connect lesbian, gay, bisexual, transgender, and queer youth around the globe. Growing up isn't easy, especially when you are trying to affirm and assert your sexual orientation and/or gender identity. It can be a challenging and isolating process—but, the good news is, no one has to do it alone. I totally met Dan Savage, the founder of the It Gets Better Project. Their videos often go viral.

- **Interested in volunteering locally?** Search for a local LGBTQ+ Community Organization that needs your help. Simply enter "LGBTQ+ volunteer opportunities in _____" and fill in the blank with your hometown. You might be surprised by the resources out there—or the lack of them. Whether you volunteer your time, talents, or money, the LGBTQ+ community appreciates you! I know that I appreciate you volunteering your time to read this. See what I did there? There aren't many "V" words to describe funny. Sorry!

◆◆◆

"Being gay is like glitter, it never goes away." ~ Lady Gaga, performer and Gay icon

W is for Welcoming Schools

Well, here We are. WOW, it sure did take a While to get Where We are now. WHEW! The Wonderful news is that every school has an opportunity to be a Welcoming School, but sadly (wah wah, sad trombone music) not all of them are. Why am I highlighting this program for the letter "W?" Well, let's read on and find out together! WHEEEEEEEE! And you're Welcome!

Welcoming Schools is a program from my favorite letter "H," the Human Rights Campaign's Foundation. I can remember being at the Time to Thrive Conference when the Welcoming Schools programs was just being released (Wow! Now I kind of feel old!). HRC Foundation's Welcoming Schools is the nation's premier professional development program providing training and resources to elementary school educators to:

- Embrace All Families;

- Create LGBTQ* and Gender Inclusive Schools;

- Prevent Bias-Based Bullying; and,

- Support Transgender and Non-Binary Students.

The Welcoming Schools Program includes dozens of resources for educators and parents such as:

- Responding to kid's questions about LGBTQ*

- Remote Teaching Using Welcoming School Lesson Plans

- Top Recommendations for Diverse, LGBTQ* and Gender Inclusive Books

- A video on how Welcoming Schools can help a school's climate

- Welcoming Schools t-shirts, posters, and bookmarks

*Author's note: I did not add a plus sign onto LGBTQ in this instance as that information came directly from their website: www.hrc.org.

Why is the Welcoming Schools programs so important? We who have been in the world of education understand that children are born who they truly are, unless your sister tells you you're gay when you're 27. (see my TEDx talk *"Allies Save Lives"*). Research says that children know their true selves as early as age 3, and by age 7 may be embracing their true identities.

"About one in six students who had expressed their gender in a way that was different than their sex assigned at birth, stopped going to school for a period of time due to harassment. Almost half of that group experienced homelessness as well." Jamie M. Grant et al. (2011) National Transgender Discrimination Survey.

When we welcome ALL, we all win! The sooner we learn about and practice inclusivity and how to be welcoming, the less school suspensions will happen. As I like to say, if kids don't feel safe at school, they don't attend. If they don't attend, they don't learn. If they don't learn, they might not graduate. If they don't graduate, they might not succeed in life. Welcoming schools and welcoming communities matter.

Hate is learned at home. Babies are not born homophobic; they are taught that wicked lesson. Let's not have that carry over into our schools. Bullying, anxiety, and trauma are some trigger words for our REACTIVE educational programming. Welcoming Schools from the Human Rights Campaign provides PROACTIVE educational programming and resources to make our World a Wonderful place!

◆◆◆

"The richness, beauty and depths of love can only be fully experienced in a climate of complete openness, honesty and vulnerability." ~ Anthony VennBrown, activist

"Conversion therapy" has been a major issue for LGBTQ youth for decades, or perhaps even longer. It is often used in Christian communities to encourage queer youth to use religion to combat their homosexual desires. Anthony Venn Brown underwent such therapy in Australia and later publicly denounced such programs. He advocated for the abolition of such programs by describing the damage that they do to LGBTQ youth who are forced to undergo them, as well as the damage that lack of acceptance can have on the entire community.

X is for our XXIVth Letter!

Xylophone, Xenophobia, Xena Warrior Princess, where should we start? You won't need your Xerox® machine. Don't be a Xenophobe: **Xenophobia**, from the Greek xenos, meaning "stranger" or "foreigner," and phobos, meaning "fear," is the fear or hatred of that which is perceived to be foreign or strange. Did you know there are several 15-letter words that start with the letter X? Me neither. So, how can you be an ally by knowing about the letter X? Thanks for asking! Let's Xplore!

If you haven't heard about preferred gender pronouns yet, now is the perfect time! A preferred gender pronoun, or PGP, is simply the pronoun or set of pronouns that an individual would like others to use when talking to or about that individual. Learning about and using PGPs offers opportunities for you to become a better LGBTQ+ ally and shift from a small "a" ally to a capital "A" Ally. *Xe, Xir, Xem, Xeir* and its variations are gender neutral pronouns that can be used to refer to people who are non-binary, genderfluid, genderqueer, trans, and/or don't identify with the gender binary.

Guess what? There are also pronouns that start with the letter "Z," but you'll have to wait for that information. Thanks for waiting: Zie, Zir, Zirs. Zer ya go. Zee what I did zhere? Don't forget about the courtesy title of Mx. back in chapter "N."

More about PGPs from our friends at GSAFE: "In English, the singular pronouns that we use most frequently are: I, you, she, her, he, him, and it. 'I,' 'you,' and 'it' are what we call 'gender neutral' or 'all gender.' 'She,' 'her,' 'he,' and 'him' are gendered. This can create an issue for transgender and gender nonconforming people, because others may not use the pronouns they prefer when speaking to them or about them.

Some people prefer that you use gender neutral or gender inclusive pronouns when talking to or about them. In English, the most commonly used singular gender-neutral pronouns are ze (sometimes spelled zie) and hir. 'Ze' is the subject pronoun and is pronounced /zee/, and 'hir' is the object and possessive pronoun and is pronounced /heer/. This is how they are used: 'Chris is the tallest person in class, and ze is also the fastest runner.' 'Tanzen is going to Hawaii over break with hir parents. I'm so jealous of hir.'

When in doubt about using pronouns, I was taught to say this. "Chris is taking Chris' backpack to Chris' locker." Xcellent! People might use these pronouns because they don't like their birth name, or for a variety of reasons. When in doubt, ask! If you mess up, apologize, and ask how to make it better. If they want to drop it, drop it. Do NOT keep pressuring them to make yourself feel better for messing up.

Remember: Just like sexual orientation, a person's gender identity can be a very personal and private thing. No one should ever feel pressured to share how they identify. If someone does choose to share, that's great, and that information should remain confidential within your group unless that person has specifically said that it's okay to talk about elsewhere. We should also remember that the idea of PGPs and gender neutral or gender inclusive pronouns will be a new concept to a lot of folks, and that mistakes will happen.

A great way to show your Allyship is to include your PGPs on your social media profiles like Twitter, LinkedIn, and Facebook (as of 2020). Another shift could involve writing your PGPs on your name badge the next time you go to a program or event. Even if your PGPs match your outward appearance, by including them you are showing another outward sign of support to the LGBTQ community. I use she/her in my emails, on my video calls, and again, if you're reading this in the future and we are using holograms, I'll use she/her there, too!

If you're not sure what to say to someone with pronouns that do not match yours, please click on this link from UW-Milwaukee to help you. I have included both my PGPs and a link to this information in my email signature for your inclusionary information. It appears like this under my title: She/Her/Hers What's This? When you click on "What's This." it gives you lots of pronoun usage information. Please feel free to copy it for your purposes.

"Y" not stay tuned to read the last two chapters? Xena Warrior Princess would be Xtra Proud of you. Zo would I.

◆◆◆

"I am proud that I found the courage to deal the initial blow to the hydra of public contempt." ~ Karl Heinrich Ulrichs, author and activist

Karl Heinrich Ulrichs is known as one of the first gay men to publicly announce his sexual identity. Born in Germany in 1825, his coming out was a historic and brave moment. During his lifetime, Ulrichs wrote numerous essays discussing homosexuality and asserting that non-heterosexual orientations are natural and biological. Despite being arrested numerous times, Ulrichs stated in the above quotation that he was proud of the work that he did for the LGBTQ community.

Y is for You

When it comes to the letter "Y," the most important resource I can think of is "YOU!" Yep! It's YOU, dear reader!

Margaret Mead said, *"Never doubt that a small group of thoughtful, committed citizens can change the world; indeed, it's the only thing that ever has."* Even though the word YOU isn't in the quote, You get the idea, don't You? What You say, or don't say has an impact. How You act or don't act has an impact. Where You spend your time, money, and talent—or don't spend Your precious resources—does matter!

You don't have to go to a Pride parade or wear rainbow clothing, yet You can still be an Ally in some simple, yet powerful ways. I'll remind You of three ways You can be an LGBTQ+ Ally:

1) **SHOW** You are an ally by not buying pink or blue items for a baby shower. Green, yellow, and purple are lovely non-gender-specific colors. You can SHOW you're an ally by wearing a rainbow ribbon or displaying a rainbow sticker. You will SHOW anyone in the LGBTQ+ world You are an ally by that simple gesture. Or you could leave a copy of this book on your desk or bookshelf for others to see when they visit you. You never know who needs to see that you're an Ally. That's why the book cover is a rainbow!

2) **SHIFT** Your mindset and those mindsets around You. When You hear a homophobic joke, or, if You see a homophobic meme, STOP the joke, or STOP the meme. You can SHIFT from a small "a" ally to a capital "A" Ally by shifting the hurtful behaviors around You. Sometimes silence equals approval. Let that sink in for a moment. If you're silent, You might be sending an inadvertent signal that You approve of something highly offensive. What can, and will You do? It can be scary, and I know You've got this! Yep!

3) **SHAPE** Your environment to be inclusive. You control where you spend your money or how and when you vote. Voting in local elections is just as important as voting in state-wide or national elections. You can have a voice in your school board, your Homeowners Association (HOA), or your clubs. You also decide where to volunteer. If You can SHAPE policies, that is a double bonus! If you are in any majority group, how will You use Your voice to help?

Maya Angelou said it best– *"I've learned that people will forget what you said, people will forget what you did, but people will never forget how you made them feel."* You matter. You are not alone. You can make a difference. You get the idea, right? YEP!

◆◆◆

"We should indeed keep calm in the face of difference, and live our lives in a state of inclusion and wonder at the diversity of humanity." ~ George Takei, actor, author, and activist

Z is for Safe ZONE Project training

Zo, here we are at the letter "Z" or as they say in Australia, Zed. I had Zero chance to pull off a Zippy title for this final chapter, zo, let'z just get on with this wonderful resource!

At each school I worked at, I displayed a Safe Zone sticker in my office. There was always a rainbow on the sticker, a symbol to the LGBTQ+ community, indicating I was a safe person and that my office was a safe place/Zone. My first Safe Zone stickers came from GLSEN (Gay Lesbian Straight Education Network) which we've already discussed. Let's dive into the Safe Zone Project and their free resources.

Right from their website: The Safe Zone Project *(SZP) is a free online resource providing curricula, activities, and other resources for educators facilitating Safe Zone trainings (sexuality, gender, and LGBTQ+ education sessions), and learners who are hoping to explore these concepts on their own. Co-created by Meg Bolger and Sam Killermann in 2013, the SZP has become the go-to resource for anyone looking to add some Safe Zone to their life.* I totally told them I was putting them in the book, and they were excited!

Check out even more from their website filled with FREE, uncopyrighted, gifts! "All of the material on The Safe Zone Project is offered in the spirit of the gift: this means there are no paywalls, everything is freely accessible, and even uncopyrighted."

Yep! They released their copyright on all of their creative works on their site. That means you can use their materials however you'd like, whenever you'd like, and with whomever you'd like; you can change them, make them your own, and that's all good with the developers. In fact, it's encouraged! Cool, right??

The Safe Zone Project has articles, FAQs, activities, and courses for learners. I think I counted a Zillion different free resources. Zust kidding, but zeriously, zey have lotZ.

◆◆◆

"If I wait for someone else to validate my existence, it will mean that I'm shortchanging myself." ~ Zanele Muholi, activist and artist

Zanele Muholi is a South African activist and artist. She works primarily in photography and video. Despite her fame as an artist, Muholi identifies herself as an activist first. It is her intention to use her art to highlight the beauty and individuality of black LGBTQ women: a group that she believes has been terribly underrepresented in all forms of art. So, instead of waiting for someone else to validate LGBT women of color, she took it upon herself to bring the struggles, needs, and beauty of these women to light.

Zee end of Be an Inclusion Ally: ABCs of LGBTQ+.

Calendar for LGBTQ+ Allies

Add these dates to your calendar to be an Inclusion ALLY! Please let me know if I have missed any, and I'll add them to my next book. Thanks!

January

GLSEN No Name-Calling Week is usually around the third week in January. Gay Lesbian Straight Education Network's No Name-Calling Week is a week organized by K-12 educators and students to end name-calling and bullying in schools. Founded in 2004.

Holocaust Remembrance Day is January 27. A day to remember all the victims of the Nazi era—including the gay men killed in concentration camps. Holocaust Remembrance started in 1953. The pink triangle labeled gays in concentration camps, similar to the way the yellow Star of David labeled people of Jewish heritage. The pink triangle has been reclaimed by the LGBT community as a symbol of gay pride.

February

LGBT History Month (UK) Founded across the pond in 2005.

National School Counseling Week is always the first week of February. When I was a school counselor my experience was that most LGBTQ kids will come out to a school counselor.

National Black HIV/AIDS Awareness Day is observed each year on February 7, to increase HIV education, testing, treatment and involvement in African-American communities.

Aromantic Spectrum Awareness Week takes place the week following Valentine's Day. Aromantics are people who do not experience romantic attraction. During the week, LGBTQ groups worldwide hold events to raise awareness of aromanticism and show support for people on the aromantic spectrum.

International Stand Up to Bullying Day is the third Friday of November and last Friday of February.

March

Bisexual Health Awareness Month started in 2014. Also referred to as #BiHealthMonth; celebrated to raise awareness about the bisexual+ community's social, economic, and health disparities, advocate for resources, and inspire actions to improve bi+ people's well-being.

LGBT Health Awareness Month: Health care people, did you know this? Often LGBT people avoid the healthcare system due to past harassment or perceived stigma from mainstream healthcare providers. This is a great time to proactively reach out to the LGBT community to create a more welcoming space.

Zero Discrimination Day is March 1. #Zero Discrimination Day is observed to bring awareness that you can't get sick from interacting with people who have AIDS, that everybody should have "access to health care safely and live life fully with dignity," as per Michel Sidibé, UNAIDS Executive Director. The day is also used to bring attention to acceptance of non-straight fellow humans and not marginalize, discriminate or act cruelly against them, yet to instruct oneself, e.g. the gender continuum.

National GLBT Health Awareness Week is a nationwide event, sponsored by the National Coalition for LGBT Health, during the last week of March that promotes the health and wellness needs of the LGBTQ community.

International Transgender Day of Visibility is held each year on March 31. This day is dedicated to celebrating transgender people and raising awareness of discrimination faced by transgender people worldwide. Transgender activist Rachel Crandall founded the event in 2009.

April

National Youth HIV & AIDS Awareness Day is April 10.

Day of Silence, held mid-April, is the Gay, Lesbian and Straight Education Network's (GLSEN) annual day to protest the bullying of LGBT students and their supporters. The day-long vow of silence represents the silencing of LGBT students and their allies. Day of Silence started in April 1996. The actual celebration day varies from year to year.

Lesbian Visibility Day on April 26, celebrates, recognizes, and raises the visibility of lesbians. The National Coalition for LGBT Health first organized it. Lesbian Visibility Day started in 2008.

May

National Physical Education & Sports Week/Trans Athlete Awareness Week. Held annually during the first week in May.

International Day Against Homophobia, Transphobia, and Biphobia, observed on May 17 to raise awareness of anti-LGBT violence and repression worldwide. International Day Against Homophobia, Transphobia and Biphobia started in 2005.

Harvey Milk Day began in 2010. It honors the assassinated politician and LGBT rights activist on his birthday, May 22. It's officially celebrated in Milk's home state of California.

Irish Marriage Referendum is celebrated annually on May 22 since being founded in 2015. Ireland became the first country to legalize marriage equality through plebiscite (the direct vote of all the members of an electorate on an important public question such as a change in the constitution) on this day.

Pan (Pansexual and Panromantic) Visibility Day. May 24. Founded in 2015, this is an annual day to celebrate, recognize, and bring visibility to pansexual people.

June

LGBT Pride Month. While Pride celebrations occur year-round, June is celebrated as LGBT Pride Month in honor of the Stonewall riots, which started on June 28, 1969. June is also the month that same-sex marriage was legalized in the United States.

QTPoC Pride Week. First Week of June celebrates Queer Trans People of Color.

Pulse Night of Remembrance commemorates the loss of 49 people in the Pulse Nightclub shooting in Orlando, Florida, on June 12, 2016.

Stonewall Riots Anniversary. June 28, 1969. This is a day to remember the Stonewall Riots which are described as the start of the Trans and Gay Liberation Movement in the United States. It's a day for people to remember the biracial lesbian and drag king Stormé DeLarverie whose scuffle with the police started the rebellion.

July

International Non-Binary People's Day on July 14 was started in 2012. The date chosen due to being between International Men's Day and International Women's Day.

International Drag Day. Created by Adam Steward in 2009 and celebrated on July 16, International Drag Day gives drag artists a chance to showcase their creativity and contributions to gay culture.

August

Wear it Purple Day. Australia celebrates the final Friday of August as Awareness Day especially for young people. Founded in 2010.

September

National Suicide Prevention Week is the first week of September. From the Trevor Project, "Suicide is the 2nd leading cause of death in young people ages 10 to 24. LGB youth seriously contemplate suicide at almost three times the rate of heterosexual youth, and LGB youth are almost five times as likely to have attempted suicide compared to heterosexual youth."

Celebrate Bisexuality Day. Bisexuals and their supporters observe Celebrate Bisexuality Day on September 23 as a day to recognize and celebrate bisexuality, bisexual history, community, and culture. Started in 1999. Also referred to as BiWeek, and Bisexual+ Awareness Week Bisexual Pride Day, CBD, Bisexual Pride, and Bi Visibility Day.

Bi Awareness Week is the week leading up to Celebrate Bisexuality Day on September 23. Check GLAAD.org for specifics.

GLSEN Ally Week is around the last week in September. LOTS of free resources on GLSEN's website.

October

LGBT History Month (USA & Canada) was first celebrated in October 1994. President Barack Obama declared it a national history month in 2009. The month is intended to encourage openness and education about LGBT history and rights.

National Bullying Prevention Month is a campaign in the United States founded in 2006 by PACER's National Bullying Prevention Center. The campaign is held during the month of October and unites communities nationwide to educate and raise awareness of bullying prevention.

International Lesbian Day. October 8 and started in 1990. Annual day which celebrates lesbian culture, mainly celebrated in New Zealand and Australia.

National Coming Day is an LGBTQ awareness day observed on October 11 and encourages LGBTQ people to come out to the people in their lives as a form of personal political activism. National Coming Out Day started October 11, 1988.

On October 12, 1998, University of Wyoming student **Matthew Shepard died** after being beaten, tortured and left to die near Laramie, Wyoming four days earlier. Shepard's attackers targeted him for robbery as a gay man and pretended to be gay to lure him. Shepard's death set off a wave of protests across the country, and ultimately led to the passage of Matthew Shepard Hate Crimes Prevention Act. Shepard was interred at the National Cathedral in Washington, DC on October 26, 2018. (I have met his mom, Judy Shepard). Melissa Etheridge wrote the song, "Scarecrow" to honor Matthew Shepard.

International Pronouns Day. Third Wednesday in October and started in 2018. An annual event that seeks to make sharing, respecting and educating about personal pronouns commonplace.

Spirit Day occurs on the third Thursday in October. Started in 2010 by Canadian teenager Brittany McMillan and promoted by GLAAD (Gay & Lesbian Alliance Against Defamation), it was created in response to a series of bullying-related suicides of gay students like Tyler Clementi (Rutgers). Observers wear purple as a sign of support for LGBTQ youth.

Intersex Awareness Day commemorates the first intersex protest held on October 26, 1996, outside the American Academy of Pediatrics national conference in Boston, Massachusetts. It's an international day of grass-roots action to end shame, secrecy and unwanted genital cosmetic surgeries on intersex children.

Asexuality Awareness Week varies from year to year and occurs last full week in October started in 2010. The international campaign seeks to educate about asexual, aromantic, demisexual, and grey-asexual experiences. Asexual Awareness Week promotes awareness of those on the asexual spectrum.

November

Trans Parent Day. First Sunday in November and started in 2009. A day that celebrates life and the love between transgender parents and their children, and between parents and their transgender children.

Intersex Day of Remembrance (Intersex Solidarity Day), on November 8, marks the birthday of French intersex memoirist Herculine Barbin. The internationally observed awareness day is intended to draw attention to issues faced by intersex people.

Transgender Awareness Week typically occurs on the second week in November and celebrates and educates about transgender and gender non-conforming people and the issues associated with their transition or identity.

International Stand Up to Bullying Day is the third Friday of November and the last Friday of February.

Transgender Day of Remembrance occurs on November 20, and memorializes those murdered as a result of transphobia, and brings attention to continued violence against transgender people. Memorials typically include a reading of the names of those killed in the past year. Transgender Day of Remembrance started in 1999.

AIDS Awareness Week is the last week in November, when extra effort is made to raise AIDS awareness.

December

World *AIDS* Day takes place on December 1. Recognized by the United Nations in 1988, the day is observed to raise awareness of the HIV-AIDS pandemic, and to memorialize those lost to the disease.

Human Rights Day is celebrated annually across the world on December 10th every year.

Acknowledgements

To Lori Peacock who handed me a yellow sticky note saying, "Write that book." Here it is!

To Holly Duckworth for mapping out the plan and reminding me about Claire in the Chair. And for giving me my first podcast interview on Everyday Mindfulness. You believed in me from the beginning!

To Lisa's Book Launch Group, thank you for your suggestions and comments. Thank you, Jess Pettitt for introducing me to Robbie Samuels. Robbie, you helped me with your Mastermind plan to make this little gem of a rainbow book and a dream come true.

To my editor and friend, Laura Varela...whew, it's done! Almost 26,000 words. Who would have thought it was even possible? I admire you and hold you close to my heart.

To Kirsty Blattner for introducing me to Mary Helen Conroy, my muse and my publisher. WHEW! It's done, can you believe it? Thank you. MHC, for your tireless efforts, your suggestions, your research, your ideas, your time and your unconditional belief that this farm girl from Loganville, a suburb of Reedsburg, Wisconsin could actually write a book. You are my family and I love you not in a romantic way! MHC, Life is a Daring Adventure, and I'm not done yet...check out her books at Life is a Daring Adventure.com

To my friends and family near and far, I love you all! Especially, Angela Prestil!

Thank you, dear reader, for taking the time to read this and for Becoming an Inclusion Ally! Namaste!

A bonus tip for all of you who have read to the end of my acknowledgements. If you want to know how to win at Simon Says, just say, "Simon Says jump up." When everyone lands, they're all out. Yep! Simon never said come down. You're welcome from this old camp director!

Carol, that was for you. I can hear you saying, "YSD," you love me, and that you're proud of me! Thanks for raising me, I love you, seestor!

Lisa Koenecke (AKA)	Lady Rainbow
Littl' Lis	Lunch Lady
Kid Korner	Madi's Mama
Gauntie Lisa	Inclusion Ally
Queen Beaver	Your Everyday Gay

LISA KOENECKE

About the Author

Lisa Koenecke, M.S., is an award-winning advocate for LGBTQ + youth, a sought-after DEI consultant, an acclaimed speaker, an engaging TEDx presenter, a phenomenal Counselor Educator. She has spoken in 25 states and would love to serve your company with her brand of inclusion, humor, and engagement.

Interested in connecting with Lisa directly?

Website and blog: www.LisaKoenecke.com

Email: Lisa@LisaKoenecke.com

LinkedIn: linkedin.com/in/lisakoenecke

Thank you for finishing the book. Before you go...

- Consider a review on Amazon;

- Tweet to your favorite people;

- Share on your media;

- Buy a copy for a friend, parent, or school in need; and,

- Let people know I speak on being an Inclusion Ally.

Reviews really are golden to writers. Please take a few minutes and write one now.

I can't thank you enough for saving lives!

Lisa